CENTRAL APPALACHIAN

Wildflowers

A Field Guide to Common Wildflowers of the Central Appalachian
Mountains, Including Shenandoah National Park, the Catskill
Mountains, and the Berkshire Mountains

by Barbara Medina and Victor Medina

FALCON®

GUILFORD, CONNECTICUT
AN IMPRINT OF THE GLOBE PEQUOT PRESS

Text design: Sue Cary
Illustrations: Elizabeth Medina Gray
Photo credits: All photos by Barbara Medina unless otherwise indicated.

Library of Congress Cataloging-in-Publication Data is available.
ISBN 0-7627-1082-9

Manufactured in Korea
First Edition/First Printing

CAUTION

Ingesting plants or plant parts poses a potentially extreme health hazard and could result in sickness or even death. No one should attempt to use any wild plant for food or medicine without adequate training by a fully qualified professional. The author, publisher, and all others associated with the production and distribution of this book assume no liability for the actions of the reader.

All participants in the recreational activities suggested by this book must assume responsibility for their own actions and safety. The information contained in this guidebook cannot replace sound judgement and good decision-making skills, which help reduce risk exposure; nor does the scope of this book allow for disclosure of all the potential hazards and risks involved in such activities.

Learn as much as possible about the recreational activities in which you participate, prepare for the unexpected, and be cautious. The reward will be a safer and more enjoyable experience.

DEDICATION

We dedicate this book with love to our hiking buddies Janet, Laura, and Joseph, who as children and as adults added excitement and joy to our family wildflower jaunts. We are grateful for their inspiration.

ACKNOWLEDGMENTS

We thank the national, state, county, and regional agencies of the Central Appalachian Mountains who protect our parks, forests, and the environment. The staffs provided maps, answered our questions, and were very helpful whenever we needed guidance. The National Park Service and Forest Service as well as the state and county park and forest managers from Connecticut, Maryland, Massachusetts, New Jersey, New York, Pennsylvania, Virginia, and West Virginia were very supportive whether we contacted them by telephone, on the Internet, or at the various visitors or interpretive centers. Without their guidance this book would have not been possible. We've included agency, park, and forest addresses, phone numbers, and Internet addresses at the end of this book.

We particularly thank the staffs of the Maryland National Capital Park and Planning Nature Centers in Montgomery County, Maryland. They all have been helpful. Also we especially thank the staff of Brookside Nature Center who allowed us to select two slides from their wildflower slide collection for use in this book. Thanks also to Mara Meisel, park ranger at Shenandoah National Park.

We also thank our editor, Erin Turner, and copyeditor, Erika Serviss, for their hard work and attention to detail on this book.

We also want to thank Janet Medina, who contributed one of her slides for use in this book, Elizabeth Medina Gray for her wonderful line drawings, and Brian Gray for his guidance of the drawing project and labeling of the drawings.

CONTENTS

PREFACE

Wild plants have long had a place in legend, poetry, medicine, and dinner. Hunting for them, knowing how to identify them, and having some knowledge of their origins and uses adds to the pleasure of a day outdoors, whether in pristine forests, mountain meadows, or urban lots. This book will enable the reader to increase his or her enjoyment of wildflowers by learning where and when to find and how to identify some of the common wildflowers growing in the Central Appalachian Mountains from the Berkshires in Massachusetts and the Catskills in New York to the mountains in northern Virginia and West Virginia. Herbaceous plants as well as some of the shrubs that provide seasonal splashes of color and which are most likely to be seen on drives or walks through this region are also included.

The interchange of plants, animals, and insects across continents was initiated in the New World by the arrival of Columbus and continues to this day. As increasing numbers of settlers arrived on these shores, they often brought along plants from their original homes. Flooding rivers, roaming animals, humans, birds, and the wind all did their share to distribute these alien seeds throughout North America. The environment determined how well these new plant arrivals prospered and competed with native plants already in place. Thus, plants whose early origins are known to be in Europe or Asia are now also found in parts of the Central Appalachians as well as other parts of North America.

The history of humans and plants on this planet speaks eloquently to the interdependence of the two. Every vegetable, fruit, and grain commonly part of our diet is a descendant of wild plants, and in some cases the wild plants themselves are still consumed. Herbal medicine dates back to the earliest history of humans, and today the great majority of people on this planet rely on traditional medical practices in which herbal medicine is an important part. In the United States just a few generations ago, the useful properties of aniseroot, wild mustard, boneset, colic root, and dozens of other plants were well known and many rural homes kept an ample supply of these drying in the attic ready for use in cooking or home medicines. Even today the derivation of modern pharmaceutical agents from plants is an expanding science rather than a lost art. Although we make reference to some plants that have been used for medicine or food, we caution against the ingestion of wild plants by the casual wildflower enthusiast. The selection of these is best left to experts. A serious error in the selection of plants for internal consumption, whether for food or medicine, can result in toxic effects, some of which can be serious.

Planting wildflowers along highways and in home gardens in a commendable effort to beautify America has become increasingly popular; however, we advise against the collection of wildflowers from their native habitats. Many of these plants thrive only in their special places, and transplantation to a home garden is often unsuccessful. Also, unrestrained removal of plants from the wild simply adds to the list of endangered plant species. Such a destructive practice is also illegal on federal lands and in most state and county parks. A number of reputable nurseries supply seeds and plants that have not been derived from stock taken out of the wild.

Many states, through the agencies responsible for protecting the environment or managing state parks and forests, maintain inventories of wild plants. These agencies welcome information on where and when less common wildflowers have been found. Contact information for these agencies and the parks where we have identified these wildflowers is found at the back of this book. Park staff can forward the information to the proper agency.

The common names for wildflowers vary with historic period and geographic region. As a result, some plants can have a list of more than a half dozen common names, none of which resemble each other. The more precise or scientific naming method uses botanical names, generally derived from Latin or Greek terms that botanists first methodically developed some three hundred years ago. The system relies on the use of two names for a plant, the scientific genus and species names. However, although not nearly as variable as the common name problem, botanical names for wildflowers are also not always agreed upon. In order to be consistent with botanical names and common names, we use the nomenclature adopted by the field guides most used in the eastern United States. The botanical names come from *Gray's Manual of Botany*, eighth edition.

The colors of wildflowers are not always exactly the same shade for the same flower all the time in every place. Some flowers naturally grow in more than one color or shade, or may even be multicolored; we will point these out in our plant descriptions. The color of a flower may also vary when viewed in the field or in photographs. These disparities most affect flowers that are in the pink-to-red or lavender-to-blue or purple color ranges. To help the viewer quickly find flowers in these color ranges, we have put those few flowers that are almost always red, orange, or blue into those color categories and put all others in the more variable pink/purple color category.

With many wildflowers, getting closer means seeing more. We recommend taking along a magnifying glass on woodland walks. Those prepared to get down on their knees to peer at these flowers through a lens are in for a treat.

INTRODUCTION

The Appalachians

Eastern North America is a landscape of extreme variety—plains, mountains, and coastal lands all serve as habitat for thousands of species of wildflowers. Within this landscape sits a narrow, continuous chain of mountains and valleys known to geologists as the Appalachian Province. This entire Appalachian chain stretches over 2,000 miles from Newfoundland to Alabama, roughly paralleling the east coast of North America, and includes some of the most splendid continuous geological features of eastern North America. For purposes of clarity and to avoid confusion, we point out that the Appalachians also cut through a region known as "Appalachia," a name which is often used to describe the region's people, their arts, customs, and lands; it is not a substitute name for the chain of the Appalachians.

The plate tectonics theory helps explain how continents were formed and how they changed over geological time. As pieces of the earth's crust moved, collided, and folded over eons, they formed mountains. Evidence from rocks shows that these rifting and collision processes have been going on for more than 2 billion years.

The North American landmass itself was formed by a series of massive movements of the earth's crust, the last of which ended about 1 billion years ago. Some 250 to 500 million years ago three separate, massive movements of the crust took place in eastern North America, and the Appalachians were formed. Over time these Appalachians were subjected in part to the modifying actions of glaciers and erosion by wind and water, resulting in the chain of mountains and valleys we see today.

Within the boundaries of the entire Appalachian chain we find mountains that themselves have their own well-known and distinctive names, such as the Great Smoky Mountains, the Blue Ridge Mountains, the Catskills, the White Mountains, the Berkshires, and the Green Mountains, to name just a few.

The Central Appalachians

In this book we concentrate on the wildflowers of the section called the Central Appalachians, which run through parts of Virginia, West Virginia, Maryland, Pennsylvania, New Jersey, New York, Connecticut, and Massachusetts. Starting at the southern terminus of Shenandoah National Park in Virginia, leading northeast into the Catoctin Mountains of Maryland and through West Virginia, the range moves through Pennsylvania and the New Jersey highlands, then into New York. In the Hudson highlands of New York, Bear Mountain and Harriman Park lands are warmed by the nearby Hudson River and form a transition zone between the oak and hickory forests to the south and the hemlocks and northern hardwoods growing in the Catskills, Berkshires, and beyond.

The region in which the Central Appalachians sit has several distinct physical zones running east-west from the ocean to the mountains. The Coastal Plain extends from the continental shelf westward, rising to meet the Piedmont Plateau at a point called the fall line. This Piedmont Plateau is a hilly region extending west from the fall line at the western edge of the Coastal Plain to meet the Blue Ridge region. The Piedmont ranges from 30 to 50 miles wide and stretches north to south from southern New York to Alabama, reaching a maximum height of 800 feet. The Blue Ridge region begins at the western edge of the Piedmont as a series of low hills in southern Pennsylvania, but quickly stretches south to the mountains of Shenandoah National Park with heights of more than 4,000 feet. The slopes of the Blue Ridge are covered with many streams flowing either east or west. The mountain streams on the east side run into the Piedmont region and then through tributaries of the Potomac and Rapahannock Rivers feeding Chesapeake Bay and flowing into the sea. The streams on the western side run into the Shenandoah River and then run northward into the Potomac River. The great variety of plant life in the Blue Ridge is surpassed only by that in the Great Smoky Mountains to the south. West of the Blue Ridge lie the gently rolling hills and valleys of the Great Valley, about 15 to 25 miles wide, and stretching from New York south to Alabama. West of the Great Valley lies the Valley and Ridge zone, with valleys between ridges as high as 3,000 feet. Finally, the western boundary of the Appalachian Mountains is at the

Allegheny Plateau, which abuts the Valley and Ridge zone. Moving westward, the Allegheny Plateau rises to 3,000 feet and then slopes gradually into the flatter areas of midwestern America. This plateau forms the continent's eastern drainage divide with rivers on the west side reaching the Gulf of Mexico via the Ohio and Mississippi Rivers, while waters from the east side run into the Atlantic ocean via Chesapeake Bay.

The geological history of a region has a great effect on the types of plants that thrive there. Soil type and topography are key factors in determining the amount of moisture retained by the soil, and in this region we find an entire spectrum of dry (xeric), well-drained (mesic), and wet (hydric) habitats. The moisture content of soil and the acidity of water reaching plant roots vary with the physical and chemical nature of the soil. Limestone-rich soils can support large quantities of wildflowers and ferns, while exposed granite outcrops weather slowly and produce a thin, acid soil low in nutrients that will support sparse populations of a few hardy plants. Water moves downhill and, everything else being equal, leaves the tops of hills and mountains drier than the bottomlands. Moderating this will be the percolating properties of the soil and bedrock. Coarse soil drains moisture more quickly than fine soils. Also, the porosity of the bedrock will govern whether more or less water will accumulate in the soil above. The weather at the top of a 4,000-foot mountain will be quite different than the weather in the valley below at the same time of year and at the same latitudes, affecting the plant life within the same Appalachian mountain group. All these factors are at work in the Central Appalachians.

These mountains have hosted humans for more than 10,000 years, and they continue to be a favorite of hikers and naturalists. In this Central Appalachian region we find habitats that include meadows, bogs, and forests scattered from valley floor to ridge tops. These mountains and valleys share common geological origins, and they are home to an extraordinary diversity of wildflowers.

How to Use This Book

This wildflower guide focuses on the plants of the Central Appalachian Mountains rather than on wildflowers growing in one state or a large, diverse region. The Central Appalachian Mountains range from the Catskills of New York and Berkshires of Massachusetts south to northern Virginia and West Virginia.

The entire Appalachian Mountains, from Labrador to Georgia and Alabama, share many of the same geological origins and contain some of the most splendid ecosystems in the eastern United States. The latitude, geology, amount of annual rainfall and other climatic factors, and the drainage of the river systems in these mountains determine which plants grow in each part of the chain.

Starting in early April at the southern end of the chain in Alabama and ending sometime in late June or early July at the northern end, flowering small trees and bushes provide brilliant displays along the roads that wind throughout these mountains. This guide includes many of these bushes, vines, and small trees, as well as those wildflowers that grow in the woods and other habitats of the mountains.

Many plants such as wild azaleas and wild orchids bloom only for a week or two. In the mountains, altitude as well as latitude influence when these plants bloom. Every thousand feet you go up a mountain is equivalent to going 100 miles north. As a result, some plants will bloom up to six weeks earlier at low altitudes in northern Virginia than will the same plant in northern Pennsylvania or the Catskills. In order to help the user of this guide see these limited floral displays, we have included more precise information on when they bloom throughout the Appalachian chain and some specific sites where they can be found. There is also a section in the back of the book that details how to contact these sites to get additional information.

The section of the book that illustrates and describes the plants separates flowers by color. Flowers that have more than one color or that range in color appear in the section of the dominant color in the illustration, and the text describes any other colors associated with the flowers of this plant. Within the section of a given color, flowers are then sorted alphabetically into groups by their botanical family name and then further ordered alphabetically by genus and species within each family.

The accompanying description gives first the common name of the flower, which is the name or names most frequently used in the region where the plant grows. It is usual for a plant to have a number of common names. Many of these common names relate to the supposed properties of the plant, others to their habitat or appearance. The botanical name of the flower is given next in italics, with the generic name first, followed by the species. The family is then listed with the common family name followed by the botanical family name in parentheses. The botanical name of each plant is also usually descriptive of the appearance of the plant but uses Greek or Latin terms.

The **Description** provides visual cues essential to identifying the plant: plant height, the shape and placement of leaves, flower size, and the shape and color of petals. Other distinguishing characteristics such as wings (thin flaps at the edge of a leafstalk or along a stem or other part of the plant) and whether the plant is classified as a vine or a bush are also included as necessary. We used as few technical terms in the description as possible. However, there are accepted standard names for the parts of the plant and for some distinguishing characteristics of leaves, flowers, and other plant parts. We have used these terms when it helps distinguish one plant from similar ones. A glossary of standard botanical terms used in this guide is at the end of the book.

If the stem of the entire plant or the stalk of a leaf or a flower provides distinguishing characteristics of the plant, it is described. Plants can have leaves on their stem, at the base of the plant, or both at the base and on the stem. Stem leaves can be opposite each other, alternate on the stem, or grow in a circular arrangement and form what is called a **whorl.** Noticing leaf placement helps distinguish those plants that have flowers that are similar in shape and color but differ in the placement and shape of their leaves. For example dandelions *(Leontodon)* and hawkweeds *(Hieracium)* have similar

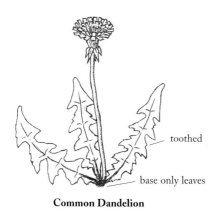

Common Dandelion

toothed

base only leaves

alternate

toothed

lance-shaped leaves

Hawkweed

yellow flowers, but their leaf placement and shape differ enough to allow positive identification.

In describing leaf shape, the term **entire** refers to a continuous and unbroken outer margin. **Toothed** describes the leaf with pointed breaks in the margin. **Lobed** refers to rounded breaks. A leaf that is cut one or more times is called **divided,** and its parts are called **leaflets.** If it is so finely divided that it resembles a fern, the leaf is described as **fernlike.** Yellow Wood Sorrel *(Oxalis stricta)* and Dwarf Cinquefoil *(Potentilla canadensis)*

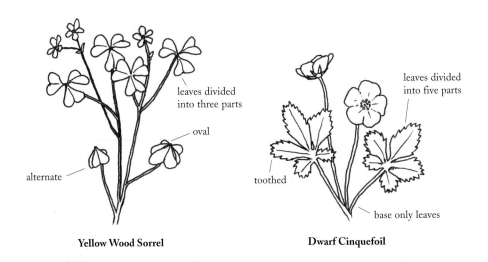

leaves divided into three parts

oval

alternate

leaves divided into five parts

toothed

base only leaves

Yellow Wood Sorrel   **Dwarf Cinquefoil**

both have yellow flowers with five petals, but the Sorrel leaves are divided into three rounded leaflets, while the Cinquefoil has five toothed leaflets.

Flowers are usually the showiest part of the plant, and the flower descriptions emphasize the shape, number of petals, size, and color. Other descriptive terms for parts of the flower such as the **calyx** and **corolla** are sometime used. The outer colored part, the **petals,** all together form the **corolla,** and the outer leaflike parts of the flower, called **sepals,** make up the **calyx.** Occasionally the reproductive parts of a flower, the male **stamen** and **pollen** or female **ovary, pistil,** and **stigma,** are mentioned when these parts can be used to distinguish one flower from another. There are also a few plants that have tiny flowers growing on a stalk shaped like a club, called a **spadix,** which is enclosed in a partial hood called a **spathe.**

Composite Flower

Lipped Flower

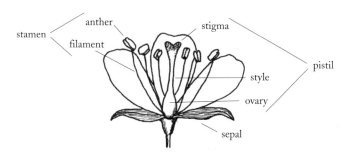

Reproductive System

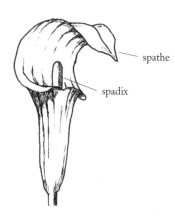

Jack-in-the-Pulpit

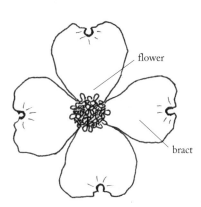

Flowering Dogwood

Most flowers described in this book are symmetrical or have a unique shape, such as when one petal forms a protruding lip, or when a mass of flowers forms a head in which the parts of the flower cannot be distinguished one from the other. Flowers can be regular, with **rays, petals,** or **bracts** (which look like petals) arranged in a symmetrical pattern, each similar to all others in shape. A bract can have almost any shape and look like a leaf or petal of a flower. The bracts of a plant are identified in the description only when they can be mistaken for a petal in a regularly shaped flower, as in the Dogwood *(Cornus florida)*, or mistaken for an identifying leaf. In the composite family, the **rays,** which themselves are flowers, circle the disk, which is the center of the flower head. The daisy is a commonly found example of a composite.

Bloom Season indicates the time of year one is most likely to see the flowers at some location in its range.

The **Habitat/Range** section provides information on the environment (woods, open places, marshes, etc.) in which the plant is generally found and the entire range of locations where it has been seen.

The **Comments** section provides a variety of information, some of which can aid in the identification of plants of the same genus that are not illustrated in this guide. Some plants in the Appalachian Mountains may differ visually from the species illustrated in this guide by something as simple as the shape of the leaf. Many different kinds of violets and goldenrods fall into this category. The comment section lists some of these plants and describes their unique characteristics. For plants that are less common or that bloom for a short period of time and whose bloom season varies from one location to another, specific site locations and bloom times are provided. When a location is listed for these plants, it is not the only spot where the plant may be found, but simply one of many. Whether a plant is commonly used for food and medicine or special information about the common or botanical name of the plant is also noted in the comments section.

Finding Good Wildflower Hunting Sites and Times

At the back of the book, the "Places Cited" section lists the locations of the various places appearing under **Comments** where we have seen these flowers. We also list addresses, phone numbers, and Web Sites for these areas.

These contacts are the best way to find out about road and weather conditions and particularly about which wildflowers are in bloom. We've also provided the e-mail addresses for the federal and state agencies responsible for management of the parks and forests in the Central Appalachian region.

We also include a list of additional reading for those wishing to delve deeper into the subject.

The Wildflowers

WHITE FLOWERS

Giant Rhododendron

Water Willow

WATER WILLOW
Justicia americana
Acanthus Family (Acanthaceae)

Description: The narrow, lanceolate leaves are opposite each other on the stem of this 1–3' plant. The ½–¾" white flowers have purple spots and 1 of the 4 petals forms a lip.

Bloom Season: July–August

Habitat/Range: Grows in wet places from Quebec to Michigan and south to Texas and Georgia.

Comments: Water Willow is often found in the water or along the gravelly or sandy banks of rivers or streams that flood. On Pine Creek in Pennsylvania it is found in the gravelly banks. The beautiful flower can be best appreciated when viewed through a magnifying glass.

BROAD-LEAVED ARROWHEAD OR COMMON ARROWHEAD
Sagittaria latifolia
Water Plantain Family (Alismataceae)

Description: The arrow-shaped leaves at the base of this 8–18" water plant can be broad or narrow. The 1–2" flowers have 3 white petals.

Bloom Season: July–September

Habitat/Range: Arrowheads grow at the edge of streams, rivers, and ponds. Common Arrowhead is found throughout North America and as far south as Mexico.

Comments: This plant is also known as Duck Potato because of the white starchy part of the root of the plant. These "potatoes" were eaten and relished by numerous Native Americans from the Pacific Coast to the Atlantic Coast.

Broad-Leaved Arrowhead or Common Arrowhead

Poison Ivy

POISON IVY
Toxicodendron radicans
Sumac Family (Anacardiaceae)

Description: Poison Ivy leaves can vary in shape. Sometimes they are toothed ovals, and sometimes they can look like small oak leaves, but the leaves are always arranged in a group of 3 on the stem of this vine. When the leaves are young, they are often shiny and reddish. As the vine matures, the leaves turn green, and in moist locations with a long growing season, the leaves can be very large. The vine is covered with hairs. The tiny flowers have 5 greenish white petals and grow in a cluster. The berries are white.

Bloom Season: May–June

Habitat/Range: In trees and thickets and along fences from Nova Scotia to British Columbia and south to Florida and Texas. The vine is less frequently found north of central Pennsylvania. It is everywhere in the woods in states south of the Mason–Dixon Line.

Comments: All parts of this plant are poisonous, and contact with any part of the plant can cause severe, weeping rashes on people who are sensitive to the irritant in its oil. The vine is deciduous but can be identified in winter because the thick stem is extremely hairy. Some books separate the Poison Ivy vine with oak-shaped leaves into a separate plant they call Poison Oak *(Toxicodendron toxicarium).* Whatever it is called, both vines have the same properties and should be avoided.

Spikenard

SPIKENARD
Aralia racemosa
Ginseng Family (Araliaceae)

Description: The leaves of this 3–6' plant are divided into large toothed and heart-shaped leaflets that alternate on the stem. The 1", 5-petal flowers are greenish white and form small round clusters. There are usually 2 or 3 clusters on each flower stalk. The flower stalks form a long cluster at the end of the stem.

Bloom Season: July–September

Habitat/Range: In rich woods from New Brunswick to Georgia.

Comments: Spikenard is known for its aromatic root, and Native Americans used this plant's root as a tea for a number of ailments and also used it to improve the flavor of other medicines. Spikenards are found along Pine Creek in Pennsylvania.

DWARF GINSENG
Panax trifolium
Ginseng Family (Araliaceae)

Description: The leaves of this 6–8" plant are toothed, divided in 3 sections, and form a whorl of 3 on the stem. The tiny flowers have 5 white petals, and together they form a ball.

Bloom Season: April–May

Habitat/Range: In moist woods from Nova Scotia to Georgia.

Comments: Native Americans used this plant medicinally for various ills. They made a tea from the plant, and they chewed the roots to treat headaches and fainting. However, popular ginseng products are not made from Dwarf Ginseng. This plant's medicinal uses have not been studied by modern medicine.

Dwarf Ginseng

POKE MILKWEED
Asclepias exaltata
Milkweed Family (Asclepiadaceae)

Description: The entire, elliptical, tapered leaves are opposite each other on the stem of this 3–5' plant. The ¾" drooping flowers are greenish white, and each of the 5 petals has a pointed crown and a dangling point.

Bloom Season: June–July

Habitat/Range: In dry woods from Maine to Minnesota and south to Georgia and Arkansas.

Comments: Poke Milkweed grows along the Lake Trail in Bear Mountain State Park in New York State, and on Blue Mountain and in the woods throughout Shenandoah National Park, both in Virginia.

Poke Milkweed

White Milkweed

WHITE MILKWEED
Asclepias variegata
Milkweed Family (Asclepiadaceae)

Description: The oblong leaves are opposite each other on the stem of this 1–3' field plant. The ½–¾" flowers are white with a purple-tinged center. The flowers form clusters of 5 with pointed crowns and dangling petals.

Bloom Season: May–July

Habitat/Range: In dry woods from Connecticut to Illinois and south to Florida and Texas.

Comments: This milkweed can be distinguished from the other white-flowered milkweed, Poke Milkweed, because the flower cluster is erect and there are more flowers in each cluster.

Mayapple or Mandrake

MAYAPPLE OR MANDRAKE
Podophyllum peltatum
Barberry Family (Berberidaceae)

Description: The large, toothed leaves are opposite each other on the stem of this 1–1½' plant. The 1½–2" flowers have 6–9 waxy, white petals and grow on the stem of the plant just below the long stalks of the 2 leaves.

Bloom Season: April–June

Habitat/Range: In woods from western Quebec to southern Ontario and south to Florida and Texas.

Comments: This plant comes out of the ground in early spring looking like a closed umbrella. The umbrella opens up into a plant with 1 or 2 large leaves. The flowers, and hence the fruit, are found only on plants that have 2 leaves. The fruit is edible when ripe, but the unripe fruit can cause severe digestive problems. Ripe fruit will be bright yellow in color and slightly soft. The root of the plant is poisonous.

WILD COMFREY
Cynoglossum virginianum
Borage Family (Boraginaceae)

Description: The top-clasping, lanceolate, hairy leaves alternate on the stem of this plant. The ½" flowers have 5 whitish, pale blue, or violet petals.

Bloom Season: April–June

Habitat/Range: In open woods from southern Connecticut to Illinois and south to Florida and Texas.

Comments: The open woods that surround the Hog Rock Nature Trail in Catoctin Mountain National Park, Maryland, are the ideal habitat for this plant. In the Appalachian Mountains of Maryland this plant blooms in May.

Wild Comfrey

SMOOTH ROCK CRESS
Arabis laevigata
Mustard Family (Brassicaceae)

Description: The lanceolate, toothed leaves are opposite each other and clasp the stem of this 1–3" plant. The ⅛" flowers have 4 greenish white petals and are shaped like small bells with an extended clapper.

Bloom Season: April–June

Habitat/Range: In rocky woods from Quebec to Ontario and south to Georgia and Arkansas.

Comments: This delicate plant often grows at the base of trees and can be easily overlooked. It grows in late May in western Pennsylvania and in West Virginia.

Smooth Rock Cress

Toothwort or Crinkleroot

TOOTHWORT OR CRINKLEROOT
Dentaria diphylla
Mustard Family (Brassicaceae)

Description: The leaves are divided into 3 toothed, ovate leaflets. There are 2 leaves opposite each other on the stem of this 8–15" plant. The ½–1" bell-shaped flowers have 4 white petals.

Bloom Season: April–May

Habitat/Range: In rich woods and meadows from Nova Scotia and New Brunswick to Minnesota and south to South Carolina and Kentucky.

Comments: Native Americans used the fresh crushed leaves of this plant or a tea from the leaves to ease poison-ivy rash. Ironically, in some people contact with the plant will cause skin irritation.

CUT-LEAVED TOOTHWORT OR PEPPERROOT
Dentaria laciniata
Mustard Family (Brassicaceae)

Description: The leaves are finely divided and toothed. The leaves form whorls of 3 on the stem of this 6–12" plant. The ½–1" flowers have 4 white or pink petals and are bell-shaped.

Bloom Season: March–June

Habitat/Range: In moist or rich woods from Quebec to Florida and west to Minnesota.

Comments: Cut-Leaved Toothwort is the most common of the toothworts found in the Appalachian Mountains. Native Americans ate the peppery-tasting rhizomes (roots) of this plant. The leaves are edible also, and some people prefer pepperroot leaves and roots to other greens and potatoes.

Cut-Leaved Toothwort or Pepperroot

JAPANESE HONEYSUCKLE
Lonicera japonica
Honeysuckle Family (Caprifoliaceae)

Description: The ovate leaves are opposite each other on this vine. The ¾–1" flowers have 5 white petals that turn yellow as they age.

Bloom Season: May–September

Habitat/Range: Escaped from cultivation and is found from Connecticut to Florida.

Comments: Japanese Honeysuckle flowers give off a pleasant sweet smell in the evening and the plant blooms almost all of the growing season in the Appalachian Mountains. In spite of its attributes, it is one of least desirable plants found in undeveloped areas. It will grow under almost any conditions of light and moisture and it kills trees and native wildflowers by cutting off their sunlight.

Japanese Honeysuckle

Common Elder

COMMON ELDER
Sambucus canadensis
Honeysuckle Family (Caprifoliaceae)

Description: The shiny leaves on this 4–7' shrub or small tree are divided into 5–10 paired leaflets. The leaflets are each elliptical or lanceolate and toothed. The ¼", 5-petal flowers are white and form a flat cluster.

Bloom Season: June–July

Habitat/Range: In moist soils from Nova Scotia to Florida and west to Manitoba and Texas.

Comments: The fruit of this shrub is used to make elderberry wine, the drink made infamous in the movie and play *Arsenic and Old Lace.*

Dockmackie or Maple-Leaved Viburnum

DOCKMACKIE OR MAPLE-LEAVED VIBURNUM
Viburnum acerifolium
Honeysuckle Family (Caprifoliaceae)

Description: The maplelike leaves, which are slightly rounded at the base, are opposite each other on the stem of this 3–6' shrub. The ¼" flowers have 5 white petals and form a flat cluster about 2–3" wide. The stamens protrude up from the petals.

Bloom Season: May–June

Habitat/Range: In dry and rocky woods from New Brunswick to southern Ontario and south to Georgia and Mississippi.

Comments: The fruits of this plant ripen in September or October shortly before the leaves turn from pinkish to a very attractive magenta. This native shrub is a popular ornamental bush in suburban gardens, but it should be obtained only from a nursery that does not gather its plants from the woods.

SQUASHBERRY
Viburnum edule
Honeysuckle Family (Caprifoliaceae)

Description: The shiny, sharp-toothed, and shallowly lobed leaves are opposite each other on the branch of this 1–4' shrub. The ¼" flowers have 5 white petals and form a small, flat, 1–2"-wide cluster.

Bloom Season: May–August

Habitat/Range: In woods and thickets and along roadsides from Labrador to Alaska and south to northern New York State.

Comments: This is a shrub that prefers northern climates, though it does grow above 3,000' in elevation in northern Virginia. Each 1,000' rise in elevation is equivalent to going 100 miles north in terms of plant and animal habitat. Using this rule of thumb, a 3,000' elevation in northern Virginia would be hospitable for plants that also grow in the southern tier region of northern New York State.

Squashberry

ARROWWOOD
Viburnum recognitum
Honeysuckle Family (Caprifoliaceae)

Description: This 4–10' shrub has heart-shaped, sharply toothed, and shiny leaves that are opposite on the stem. The ¼" white flowers have 5 petals and form an umbel.

Bloom Season: May–June

Habitat/Range: Arrowwood grows in moist soils in woodlands from New Brunswick, Canada, south to the mountains of Georgia and west in the northern United States to Minnesota.

Arrowwood

Comments: Some references list Arrowwood as *Viburnum dentatum*. Others separate Arrowwood into a southern and northern variety, where the southern variety is *Viburnum dentatum* and the northern variety is *Viburnum recognitum*.

White Campion

WHITE CAMPION
Lychnis alba
Pink Family (Caryophyllaceae)

Description: The lanceolate leaves are opposite each other on the stem of this 1–3' plant. The 5 notched white or pinkish petals spread about 1" wide across the top of the sepals, which are united into a bladder that expands as the seeds ripen.

Bloom Season: May–September

Habitat/Range: Found in open places from Nova Scotia to Ontario and Michigan and south to Virginia.

Comments: White Campion blooms at dusk. Bladder Campion *(Silene cucubalus)* is often found along roadsides and looks very similar to White Campion. Bladder Campion usually has a more inflated calyx.

Starry Campion

STARRY CAMPION
Silene stellata
Pink Family (Caryophyllaceae)

Description: The long, ovate leaves form a whorl of 4 on the stem of this 1–3' plant. The 1–1½" flowers have 5 white, fringed petals that form a bell.

Bloom Season: July–September

Habitat/Range: In woods, thickets, and at the edge of roads from Massachusetts to North Dakota and south to Georgia and Oklahoma.

Comments: A common flower throughout the Central Appalachian Range, it can be found in the woods on the Rim Trail in Colton State Park, Pennsylvania; in Pittsfield State Forest, Massachusetts; in the thickets near Hessian Lake at Bear Mountain State Park, New York; and on the Appalachian Trail in Shenandoah National Park, Virginia.

STAR CHICKWEED OR GREAT CHICKWEED
Stellaria pubera
Pink Family (Caryophyllaceae)

Description: The long, ovate leaves are opposite each other on the stem of this 6–12" plant. The ½" flowers have bright red stamens and 5 deeply notched, white petals that form a star.

Bloom Season: March–June

Habitat/Range: In wooded areas and on rocky slopes from New York to Illinois and south to Alabama and Florida.

Comments: Common Chickweed *(Stellaria media)*, the bane of all gardeners, also grows in the Appalachian Mountains. Star Chickweed, its close relative, is such a lovely flower most gardeners would welcome it.

Star Chickweed or Great Chickweed

YARROW OR MILFOIL
Achillea millefolium
Composite Family (Compositae)

Description: The finely divided leaves alternate on the stem of this 1–3' plant. The small flowers are white or pink and form a flat umbel.

Bloom Season: June–October

Habitat/Range: Found throughout the Northern Hemisphere; it may have originated in Europe.

Yarrow or Milfoil

Comments: Yarrow was reportedly used medicinally in ancient Greece and as recently as in the Civil War to stanch battle wounds.

Pearly Everlasting

PEARLY EVERLASTING
Anaphalis margaritacea
Composite Family (Compositae)

Description: The long, narrow, lanceolate leaves alternate on the stem of this 1–2' plant. The underside of the leaves is white and woolly. The ½" flowers have many white petals and form a tuft with a yellowish center. The tufts of flowers group together in a loose umbel.

Bloom Season: July–October

Habitat/Range: Pearly Everlasting is found from Nova Scotia south to Georgia.

Comments: Sweet Everlasting *(Gnaphalium obtusifolium)* and Pearly Everlasting are similar looking plants, but each is in a different genus. Harriman State Park, about 40 miles north of New York City and on the eastern edge of the Central Appalachian Mountains, is the approximate location where an equal amount of Sweet Everlasting and Pearly Everlasting can be found. North from there, Pearly Everlasting is more common. Go south and Sweet Everlasting dominates.

Field Pussytoes

FIELD PUSSYTOES
Antennaria neglecta
Composite Family (Compositae)

Description: The lanceolate, woolly leaves have 1 prominent vein and are at the base of this 4–12" plant. The ¼" flowers are white and form 4 or 5 small heads at the top of the stem.

Bloom Season: April–May

Habitat/Range: In fields and meadows from Maine to Virginia and in the Smoky Mountains.

Comments: This plant is also called Field Cat's Foot. With a little imagination, the fuzzy little heads seem to look like an animal's paw.

FIELD CHAMOMILE OR CORN CHAMOMILE
Anthemis arvensis
Composite Family (Compositae)

Description: The finely divided leaves alternate on the stem of this 6–10" plant. The 1" flowers have white petals and a yellow disk.

Bloom Season: June–September

Habitat/Range: In fields from Nova Scotia to Virginia west to Michigan and Missouri and on the West Coast.

Comments: The plant was naturalized from Europe and can be found in and around former settlements. Field Chamomile can be found along Pine Creek in Pennsylvania and in Shenandoah National Park, Virginia. Sometimes it is mistaken for a small daisy.

Field Chamomile or Corn Chamomile

HEATH ASTER
Aster ericoides
Composite Family (Compositae)

Description: The lanceolate, long, narrow leaves alternate on the branches of the stem of this 1–5' plant. The stem branches are almost at right angles to the main stem and the flowers are at the end of the branch. The ½–¾" flowers are white.

Bloom Season: September–October

Habitat/Range: The plant blooms in fields and along roadsides from Maine to Minnesota and south to Georgia and Oklahoma.

Comments: There are other small white asters that grow in the Central Appalachian Mountains. Calico Aster *(Aster lateriflorus)* looks a lot like the Heath Aster plant, but its leaves are somewhat wider. Small White Aster *(Aster vimineus)* is similar but has a purple stem.

Heath Aster

PALE INDIAN PLANTAIN
Cacalia atriplicifolia
Composite Family (Compositae)

Description: The lobed leaves alternate on the stem of this 3–6' plant. The ½" flowers are white and form a flat cluster.

Bloom Season: July

Habitat/Range: In wooded areas from New York south to Florida.

Comments: Native Americans used the leaves of this plant as a poultice for cuts and bruises and to draw out blood or poisonous substances. In July it blooms along the edges of Skyline Drive from the northern entrance to Shenandoah National Park, Virginia, to its end at the intersection of I-64.

Pale Indian Plantain

Daisy or Ox-Eye Daisy

DAISY OR OX-EYE DAISY
Chrysanthemum leucanthemum
Composite Family (Compositae)

Description: The toothed, lobed leaves alternate on the stem of this 1–2' plant. The 2–3" flowers have white petals and a yellow disk. Each flower has 15–30 petals.

Bloom Season: May–September

Habitat/Range: In open places throughout the Appalachians, but less common in the south. It was naturalized from Europe and also grows in Asia.

Comments: Having a home wildflower garden is gaining in popularity and the Daisy, while not sweet smelling, makes a wonderful addition. It has a very long blooming season and is a long-lasting cut flower. Very few other wildflowers that grow in the Applachian Mountains have either of these characteristics.

FEVERFEW
Chrysanthemum parthenium
Composite Family (Compositae)

Description: The leaves of this 1–2' plant are divided into ovate, toothed segments that alternate on the stem. The ½–¾" flowers have many white petals and a yellow center disk. Each plant has a cluster of flower heads.

Bloom Season: June–September

Habitat/Range: Throughout the Central Appalachian Mountains.

Comments: When plants escape from cultivation, they are found first in empty lots and along roadsides. In areas like Shenandoah National Park, many of the old roads that were used by the people who lived there until the 1930s are now used as part of the trail system, and plants like Feverfew are found along these trails.

Feverfew

Daisy Fleabane or Sweet Scabious

DAISY FLEABANE OR SWEET SCABIOUS
Erigeron annuus
Composite Family (Compositae)

Description: The lanceolate leaves alternate on the stem of this 1–4' plant and have a few teeth on their margins. The ½–¾" flowers are made up of 50–100 white or pink petals surrounding a yellow disk.

Bloom Season: May–August

Habitat/Range: In meadows and open woods from Nova Scotia to British Columbia and south to Florida, Texas, and California. Naturalized in Europe.

Comments: Often mistaken for asters, which normally bloom in late summer and fall, Daisy Fleabane is a plant of late spring and summer. Other than in the most arid desert, Daisy Fleabane is the native plant most likely to be found in parks and wild places anywhere from southern Canada to the southern United States.

White Boneset or Common Boneset

WHITE BONESET OR COMMON BONESET

Eupatorium perfoliatum
Composite Family (Compositae)

Description: The lanceolate, toothed leaves unite around the stem of this 1–3' plant. The ¼" white flowers form a flat cluster.

Bloom Season: July–September

Habitat/Range: In wet places from New Brunswick, Nova Scotia, and Manitoba to Florida and Nebraska. Also found in Texas.

Comments: This plant is native to North America. Boneset was a plant commonly used in folk medicine, especially for treating a disease called "break-bone fever."

White Snakeroot

WHITE SNAKEROOT
Eupatorium rugosum
Composite Family (Compositae)

Description: The ovate, toothed leaves are on long stalks opposite each other on this 1–5' plant. The ¾" white flowers form a flat cluster.

Bloom Season: July–September

Habitat/Range: In rich woods from New Brunswick to Virginia and in the Appalachian Mountains from North Carolina to Georgia.

Comments: White Snakeroot commonly grows in the Catskill Mountains of New York, the Berkshire Mountains of Massachusetts, the state parks of Pennsylvania from Colton Point to Pine Grove, and in Shenandoah National Park in Virginia. Cattle who eat the plant develop a disease called "the trembles." Milk from infected cows causes illness, and Abraham Lincoln's mother is believed to have died from this "milk sickness."

Galinsoga or Quick-Weed

GALINSOGA OR QUICK-WEED

Galinsoga ciliata
Composite Family (Compositae)

Description: The toothed leaves are opposite each other on the stem of this 6–18" plant. The ¼" flowers have 5 white petals and a yellow disk.

Bloom Season: July–September

Habitat/Range: In open areas throughout northeastern North America.

Comments: Gardeners in the United States consider Galinsoga a pesky weed. In Asia, some groups cook and eat the plant as greens. As Galinsoga was one of the first plants to emerge after the bombing of London in World War II, the British named it Gallant Soldier.

SWEET EVERLASTING OR CATFOOT

Gnaphalium obtusifolium
Composite Family (Compositae)

Description: The lanceolate, long, and narrow leaves alternate on the stem of this 1–2' plant. The ½–¾" white flowers form several small clusters at the top of the stem.

Bloom Season: August–October

Habitat/Range: In dry, mostly open places from Nova Scotia to Florida.

Comments: Sweet Everlasting is found in the Bear Mountain, New York area of the Appalachian Mountains, and it becomes more and more common in the mountains of Maryland and Virginia. Although it is found as far north as Nova Scotia, it is more at home in the mid-Atlantic states and further south.

Sweet Everlasting or Catfoot

WILD QUININE OR AMERICAN FEVERFEW
Parthenium integrifolium
Composite Family (Compositae)

Description: The lanceolate, slightly toothed leaves alternate on the stem of this 1–5' plant. The leaves are rough and the lowest leaves have long stalks. The flowers have 5 white, tiny petals and form an umbel.

Bloom Times: June–September

Habitat/Range: In dry woodlands and prairies from New York to Minnesota and south to Georgia and Texas.

Comments: This is the only widespread species of this genus in the northeastern part of the United States. It grows in many places in Shenandoah National Park, Virginia. It particularly seems to like the growing conditions around the rock outcrops on ridges.

Wild Quinine or American Feverfew

Silverrod or White Goldenrod

SILVERROD OR WHITE GOLDENROD
Solidago bicolor
Composite Family (Compositae)

Description: The toothed leaves alternate on the stem of this 2–4' plant. The ½" white flowers form long cylindrical clusters.

Bloom Season: August–September

Habitat/Range: In dry soils from Prince Edward Island to Georgia and west to Tennessee.

Comments: Silverrod is a very common plant along the entire range of the Appalachian Mountains. A few of the many locations where it can be seen are: Vermont's Groton State Forest in the northern part of the range, New York's Catskills Mountains and Bear Mountain State Park in the Central Appalachians, and in the South along the Blue Ridge Parkway in Virginia and North Carolina.

Hedge Bindweed or Lady's Nightcap

HEDGE BINDWEED OR LADY'S NIGHTCAP
Convolvulus sepium
Morning Glory Family (Convolvulaceae)

Description: This trailing vine has alternate, lobed, arrow-shaped leaves. The bottom lobes of the leaf have blunt edges. The 1–2 " white flowers have 5 petals and are trumpet shaped.

Bloom Season: July–September

Habitat/Range: In fields and thickets from Maine to North Carolina. The plant is also found in British Columbia, Illinois, Nebraska, and New Mexico.

Comments: The meadow across the road from the Byrd Visitor Center in Shenandoah National Park, Virginia, and along the edges of the Skyline Drive, is the perfect habitat for this vine.

WHITE DOGWOOD
Cornus florida
Dogwood Family (Cornaceae)

Description: The entire, ovate leaves are opposite each other on the stem of this 6–20' small tree. What looks like a 2–4", 4-petal, white or pink flower is really made up of white or pink notched bracts. The actual flowers are in the center of the blossom.

Bloom Season: April–May

Habitat/Range: In wooded areas and along roads from Maine and Ontario to Florida.

Comments: A very common tree in the Appalachian Mountains from southern Pennsylvania to Georgia and Alabama. North of southern Pennsylvania, White Dogwood needs a very sheltered spot to survive the winters.

White Dogwood

RED OSIER DOGWOOD
Cornus stolonifera
Dogwood Family (Cornaceae)

Description: The ovate leaves have 5–7 veins and are opposite each other on the stems of this 5–10' shrub. The young stems are usually red. The ¼" white flowers form a flowering head. Each flower has 4 petals.

Bloom Season: June–July

Habitat/Range: In wet places and along streams from Newfoundland to Virginia.

Comments: Red Osier Dogwood is commonly found along creeks and rivers in the Central Appalachian Mountains. There is another shrub with a similar flowering head, called Alternate-Leaf Dogwood *(Cornus alternifolia)*, which is found in Shenandoah National Park. Alternate-Leaf Dogwood is the only dogwood whose leaves alternate on the branch of the shrub.

Red Osier Dogwood

Wild Stonecrop

WILD STONECROP
Sedum ternatum
Orpine Family (Crassulaceae)

Description: The ovate, fleshy leaves are opposite each other on the stem of this creeping plant. The ½" flowers have 4 or 5 white petals and are star shaped.

Bloom Season: April–June

Habitat/Range: On banks and rocky hills, from New York to Michigan south to Georgia and Tennessee.

Comments: In the spring Wild Stonecrop frequently grows among the rocks that border the Appalachian Trail from Massachusetts south to Georgia. The leaves of the Wild Stonecrop that grows along the trails in forests tend to be less fleshy than those on plants that grow on ledges in sunny areas, and some botanists consider these 2 varieties separate species.

Trailing Arbutus or Mayflower

TRAILING ARBUTUS OR MAYFLOWER
Epigaea repens
Heath Family (Ericaceae)

Description: The leathery, ovate leaves alternate on the stem of this creeping evergreen plant. The ½" flowers are white and bell shaped. Each flower has 5 petals.

Bloom Season: March–May

Habitat/Range: The plant is found in sandy or rocky woods. Once a common plant widely spread from Saskatchewan to Newfoundland and south to Kentucky and Florida, it is now found only in areas away from population centers. In some states it is against the law to pick or damage this plant.

Comments: Found in the woods around North Lake in the Catskills, New York. This is an endangered species in many states and sightings should be reported to the state agencies responsible for the environment. Contact information for these agencies in the Central Appalachian Mountain states can be found in the back of this book.

WINTERGREEN OR TEABERRY
Gaultheria procumbens
Heath Family (Ericaceae)

Description: The slightly toothed, shiny, ovate leaves form a whorl of 3 on the stem of this 2–6" creeping plant. The ½" flowers are white and form a bell with a waxy appearance.

Bloom Season: June–August

Habitat/Range: In wooded areas, especially under evergreen trees, from Nova Scotia south to Georgia.

Comments: Native Americans and early settlers extracted oil from this plant to use as a wintergreen flavor for foods. Today, commercial wintergreen used in gum and for flavoring is synthesized. Wintergreen is a common ground cover in the hemlock and pine woods of the Central Appalachian Mountains.

Wintergreen or Teaberry

Mountain Laurel

MOUNTAIN LAUREL
Kalmia latifolia
Heath Family (Ericaceae)

Description: The leaves on this 3–15' shrub are evergreen and shiny. The ¾", white, cup-like flowers have 5 white (at times pink tinted) petals that form a terminal cluster.

Bloom Season: June–August

Habitat/Range: In woods, preferring rocky or sandy soils, from New Brunswick to Ontario and south to Florida and Louisiana.

Comments: This beautiful but poisonous shrub can be found throughout the Appalachian Mountains. It begins to bloom in late April in Georgia and Alabama and around the first week of June in northern Virginia and the second week of June in northern Pennsylvania and New York. The woody branches should not be used for cooking food. Children can be poisoned by eating the leaves.

Smooth Azalea

SMOOTH AZALEA
Rhododendron arborescens
Heath Family (Ericaceae)

Description: The leaves of this 2–8' shrub are ovate with a hairy midrib. The 1–2" flowers have 5 white or pink flaring, aromatic petals. The red stamens extend beyond the petals.

Bloom Season: May–June

Habitat/Range: In wooded areas and swamps from Massachusetts to Ohio south to Florida and Louisiana.

Comments: Native azalea can be found blooming in June in Shenandoah National Park, Virginia. Another similar native azalea, Clammy Azalea or Swamp Honeysuckle *(Rhododendron viscosum)*, also is found in the Central Appalachian Mountains. Its flowers are sweet smelling.

GIANT RHODODENDRON OR ROSEBAY
Rhododendron maximum
Heath Family (Ericaceae)

Description: This 5–40' shrub has shiny, dark green, lanceolate leaves. The 1½–2" flowers have 5 white or pink petals and form a cluster.

Bloom Season: June–July

Habitat/Range: In wooded areas and along streams from Nova Scotia to Ontario and south to Georgia and Alabama.

Comments: Found mostly at lower elevations in the northern section of the Central Appalachian Mountains.

Giant Rhododendron or Rosebay

HIGHBUSH BLUEBERRY OR SWAMP BLUEBERRY
Vaccinium corymbosum
Heath Family (Ericaceae)

Description: The leaves on this 3–15' shrub are ovate. The ½" flowers have 5 white or pink petals in the form of a narrow bell.

Bloom Season: April–May

Habitat/Range: In swamps, thickets, and wooded areas from Maine south to Louisiana.

Comments: A great deal of the commercially grown blueberries sold in the East are the off-spring of 4 plants cultivated from the Highbush Blueberry bushes that grow abundantly in the Pine Barrens of New Jersey. Blueberry bushes are common in the Appalachian Mountains.

Highbush Blueberry or Swamp Blueberry

Flowering Spurge

FLOWERING SPURGE
Euphorbia corollata
Spurge Family (Euphorbiaceae)

Description: The entire leaves on the stem under the flowers form a whorl of 3. Below these leaves, where the stem branches, the leaves alternate on this 1–3' plant. The ¼–½" flowers have 5 white bracts that look like petals. These bracts surround the tiny flowers in a cluster.

Bloom Season: July–October

Habitat/Range: Dry fields and open, wooded areas from New York to Minnesota and south to Florida and Texas.

Comments: This plant is a relative of Poinsettia *(Euphorbia pulcherrima),* a popular houseplant at Christmastime. The flowers on the Poinsettia are similar to those on Flowering Spurge. It is those large bright red bracts on the Poinsettia that make it look so different from its much smaller relative.

Canadian Milk Vetch

CANADIAN MILK VETCH
Astragalus canadensis
Pea Family (Fabaceae)

Description: The leaves are made up of 15–32 ovate leaflets that alternate on the stalk of the leaf. The plant is between 1–4' high. The ½–¾" flowers are pea shaped and white or cream colored. There are many flowers in a thick spike.

Bloom Season: July–August

Habitat/Range: On shores and rocky banks from Vermont to British Columbia and south to Georgia, Texas, and Utah.

Comments: Canadian Milk Vetch commonly blooms in July on the rocky banks that line Skyline Drive in Shenandoah National Park. Rocky banks that abut many of the roads in the Central Appalachian Mountains are a wonderful place to look for a great many wildflowers. The rocks are wet most of the time and the little pockets of soil make a hospitable place for small flowering plants to grow. Larger plants, such as Canadian Milk Vetch, grow on rocky banks that are not as steep and have larger pockets of soil.

WHITE SWEET CLOVER
Melilotus alba
Pea Family (Fabaceae)

Description: The leaves are divided into 3 ovate leaflets that are toothed on the outer half. The leaves alternate on the stem of this 2–4' plant. The ¼–⅓", pea-shaped, white flowers form a loose vertical cluster.

Bloom Season: June–September

Habitat/Range: In fields, open places, and on roadsides throughout the United States.

Comments: White Sweet Clover is native to Europe. The plant gets its name because the leaves are fragrant when dried.

White Sweet Clover

CAROLINA VETCH OR WOOD VETCH
Vicia caroliniana
Pea Family (Fabaceae)

Description: The leaves of this vine are divided into 10–12 oblong leaflets. The leaves have a tendril at the end. The ½" flowers are white and pea shaped.

Bloom Season: May–July

Habitat/Range: In woods and on rocky slopes from Ontario to Minnesota and south to Georgia, Mississippi, and Kansas.

Comments: Vetches *(Vicia)* have a tendril at the end of their leaves to grasp. The leaves of wild peas *(Lathyrus)*—another closely related vine with pea-shaped flowers found in the Appalachian Mountains—also have this tendril at the end. There is a small technical difference between vetches and wild peas, and the wild peas' flowers are usually larger.

Carolina Vetch or Wood Vetch

Fly Poison

FLY POISON
Amianthium muscaetoxicum
Lily Family (Lilliaceae)

Description: The wide, grasslike leaves are at the base of this 1½–4' plant. The 1" flowers have 6 white petals that turn green as the flowers age. The flowers form a terminal spike.

Bloom Season: June–July

Habitat/Range: In open woods and meadows from southern New York to Missouri and south to Florida, Mississippi, and Arkansas.

Comments: In June large groups of Fly Poison can be found in the Big Meadow and the woods around Big Meadows Lodge and Skyland Lodge, as well as along the Strong Man Nature Trail in Shenandoah National Park in Virginia.

Wild Lily-of-the-Valley or Canada Mayflower

WILD LILY-OF-THE-VALLEY OR CANADA MAYFLOWER
Maianthemum canadense
Lily Family (Lilliaceae)

Description: The entire, heart-shaped leaves alternate on the stem of this 3–6" plant. The base leaf clasps the stem. The ¹⁄₁₆" flowers are white and form a small upright cluster.

Bloom Season: April–June

Habitat/Range: In moist woods and thickets from Newfoundland to the Northwest Territory and south to North Carolina, Tennessee, Iowa, and South Dakota.

Comments: This small plant often grows in large groups on the woodland floor, spreading a carpet of white blooms. It starts to bloom in late April in the Southern Appalachian Mountains, in late May in the Central Appalachian Mountains, and in late June in the Northern Appalachian Mountains. It can be found around Memorial Day in Colton Point State Park, Pennyslvania, and High Point State Park, New Jersey.

FALSE SOLOMON'S SEAL
Smilacina racemosa
Lily Family (Lilliaceae)

Description: The entire, ovate leaves alternate on the stem of this 1–1½' plant. The tiny flowers have 6 white petals and form a branched terminal cluster.

Bloom Season: April–June

Habitat/Range: In moist woods and thickets from Nova Scotia to British Columbia and south to Georgia, Missouri, and Arizona.

Comments: False Solomon's Seal blooms in late April in Georgia and Alabama. Traveling north through the Appalachian Mountains, it blooms late in May in northern Pennsylvania and in June in Maine.

False Solomon's Seal

LARGE-FLOWERED TRILLIUM
Trillium grandiflorum
Lily Family (Lilliaceae)

Description: The ovate leaves form a whorl of 3 on the stem of this 8–18" plant. The 1½–2½" white flowers have 3 petals and are bell shaped. The flowers turn pink as they age.

Bloom Season: April–June

Habitat/Range: In woods from Quebec and Ontario to Minnesota and south to North Carolina and Missouri.

Comments: An unusual display of Large-Flowered Trillium interspersed with tooth-wort and other spring flowers can be seen at Blue Mountain, Virginia, in early May.

Large-Flowered Trillium

Painted Trillium

PAINTED TRILLIUM
Trillium undulatum
Lily Family (Lilliaceae)

Description: The oval leaves form a whorl of 3 on the stem of this 1–1½' plant. The 1½–2' bell-shaped flowers have 3 petals and are white with a red center.

Bloom Season: April–June

Habitat/Range: In woods from Nova Scotia to Ontario and Wisconsin south to Georgia and Missouri.

Comments: Although occasionally found at high elevations south to Georgia, this Trillium is most commonly found in the Appalachian Mountains from northern Pennsylvania through New England.

Yucca

YUCCA
Yucca filamentosa
Lily Family (Lilliaceae)

Description: The long, entire, lanceolate leaves are at the base of this 2–6' plant. The leaves have threads on the leaf margin. The 2–3" flowers form white, 4-petal bells. The flowers form a large, showy, pyramid cluster.

Bloom Season: July–September

Habitat/Range: In sandy soils from southern Pennsylvania to Florida.

Comments: Native Americans used this plant's root in salves for skin diseases and sprains.

CRIMSON-EYED MALLOW OR ROSE MALLOW
Hibiscus palustris
Mallow Family (Malvaceae)

Description: The toothed leaves alternate on the stem of this 3–5' plant. The 5–7", white or pink, 5-petal flowers form a cup. If the flowers are white, the center of the cup is splashed with crimson.

Bloom Season: July–September

Habitat/Range: In wet places and along streams from New Hampshire to Georgia.

Comments: Some references separate the white variety of Rose Mallow from the pink and assign a different species and a limited coastal range to the white variety shown here.

Crimson-Eyed Mallow or Rose Mallow

FRAGRANT WATER LILY
Nymphaea odorata
Water Lily Family (Nymphaeaceae)

Description: The leaves are at the base of the plant. Each leaf is in the form of a circle with a cleft. The underside of the leaf is red or purple, and the leaves are shiny. The 3–5" flowers have many pink or white petals and a center grouping of yellow stamens.

Bloom Season: June–August

Habitat/Range: In ponds and other quiet waters throughout the country.

Comments: Many of the ponds and lakes in the Central Appalachian Mountains are formed by dams and are perfect habitats for not only this water lily but also for Tuberous Water Lily *(Nymphaea tuberosa)*, which looks very much like Fragrant Water Lily. The major difference is that the leaves of Tuberous Water Lily are green on both sides. The flowers of both open in the morning and last for 2 or 3 days.

Fragrant Water Lily

White Bog Orchid or Bog-Candle

WHITE BOG ORCHID OR BOG-CANDLE
Habenaria dilatata
Orchid Family (Orchidaceae)

Description: The lanceolate leaves alternate on the stem of this 1½–2' plant. The ½" flowers are white, and the spur of the flower is about the same size as the lip.

Bloom Season: June–August

Habitat/Range: In meadows, bogs, and wet woods throughout Canada and south to New Jersey, Michigan, Wisconsin, South Dakota, Colorado, and California.

Comments: This orchid likes cold winters and is often found in the mountains of the Central Appalachians at the edge of wooded areas where the ground freezes in winter.

Common Wood Sorrel

COMMON WOOD SORREL
Oxalis montana
Wood Sorrel Family (Oxalidaceae)

Description: The leaves are divided into 3 ovate leaflets that fold in half when the sun is not shining. The leaves are at the base of this 2–6" plant. The 1" flowers have 5 white petals with pink lines.

Bloom Season: May–August

Habitat/Range: In northern, cool, wooded areas from Quebec to Saskatchewan and south to Pennsylvania. Also found in the Great Smoky Mountains at higher elevations.

Comments: As the species name *montana* (mountain) hints, this Wood Sorrel is found in higher elevations of the Appalachian Mountains. While its common name is Common Wood Sorrel, it is found in far fewer locations than the yellow wood sorrels.

DUTCHMAN'S BREECHES
Dicentra cucullaria
Poppy Family (Papaveraceae)

Description: The finely divided leaves are at the base of this 6–12" plant. The ½–¾" flowers are white and have spurs at the top of the plant, which has a yellow section at the very top.

Bloom Season: March–May

Habitat/Range: In wooded areas from Nova Scotia to Minnesota and south to Georgia, Missouri, and Kansas.

Comments: Dutchman's Breeches can be found in the woods along the Potomac River as early as late March. They appear in the Appalachian Mountains of Georgia in mid-April, and in northern Pennsylvania in late May.

VICTOR MEDINA

Dutchman's Breeches

BLOODROOT
Sanguinaria canadensis
Poppy Family (Papaveraceae)

Description: The leaves have 5–9 lobes and are at the base of this 4–8" plant. The 1–1½" white flowers have 8–12 petals.

Bloom Season: March–May

Habitat/Range: In rich woods from Nova Scotia to Manitoba and south to Florida and Arkansas.

Comments: The thick rootstock of this plant, poisonous if eaten, was used to produce a bright red dye. The plants bloom for about 1 week. The time of the bloom (between March and May) depends on latitude and elevation. In the Central Appalachian Mountains of Virginia and Maryland they usually start to bloom in April.

Bloodroot

POKEWEED
Phytolacca americana
Pokeweed Family (Phytolaccaceae)

Description: The lanceolate leaves alternate on the stem of this 4–10' plant. The ¼" flowers are greenish white and form a long, loose cluster. Flower clusters and berries are often seen on a plant at the same time. The berries are black or dark purple and possibly poisonous.

Bloom Season: July–October

Habitat/Range: Grows in both shaded and open areas from Maine and Ontario to Minnesota and south to Texas and Florida.

Comments: The root of the plant is also poisonous, but the young shoots can be eaten like asparagus. Birds love the berries and spread the plant far and wide.

Pokeweed

Pale Smartweed

PALE SMARTWEED
Polygonum lapathifolium
Buckwheat Family (Polygonaceae)

Description: The grasslike, entire leaves alternate on the stem of this 1–4' plant. The tiny, 5-petal flowers are pink or white and form dense spikes.

Bloom Season: August–September

Habitat/Range: A common plant of wet places, found throughout temperate North America.

Comments: This naturalized plant came to North America from Europe, and it also grows in Asia. Water Smartweed *(Polygonum amphibium)* also grows in the Central Appalachian Mountains. Its flowers are tiny and pink and form round clusters.

VIRGINIA SPRING BEAUTY
Claytonia virginica
Purslane Family (Portulacaceae)

Description: Two long, lanceolate leaves are opposite each other on the stem of this 3–7" plant. The ½–¾", 5-petal flowers are white with pink lines. Sometimes there are so many lines the flowers look pink.

Bloom Season: March–May

Habitat/Range: In moist woods from Nova Scotia to Saskatchewan and south to Georgia, Montana, and Texas.

Comments: There is another Spring Beauty, Carolina Spring Beauty *(Claytonia caroliniana)*, that blooms in the Central Appalachian Mountains. Carolina Spring Beauty has wider lanceolate leaves. The flower is similar to Virginia Spring Beauty and it grows more often in the Southern Appalachian Mountains. Both plants grow in clumps or as a carpet on the floor of wooded areas in early spring.

Virginia Spring Beauty

INDIAN PIPE OR CORPSE PLANT
Monotropa uniflora
Shinleaf Family (Pyrolaceae)

Description: The leaves of this parasitic, 6–10" plant are white scales on the stem. The stem is white and fleshy. The 1" flowers are white or pink and resemble an inverted pipe bowl.

Bloom Season: June–September

Habitat/Range: In the leaf litter of wooded areas from Newfoundland to Alaska and south to Florida and California.

Comments: The species name, *uniflora,* means that the plant bears only 1 flower. The plant turns black as it ages. This plant is also found in Central America and Asia.

BROOKSIDE NATURE CENTER

Indian Pipe or Corpse Plant

Wood Anemone or Windflower

WOOD ANEMONE OR WINDFLOWER
Anemone quinquefolia
Buttercup Family (Ranunculaceae)

Description: The leaves are divided into 3–5 toothed leaflets and form a whorl on the stem of this 3–6" plant. The 1" flowers have 5 white or pinkish, petal-like sepals.

Bloom Season: March–May

Habitat/Range: A common woodland plant from the Atlantic Coastal Plain to the eastern mountains.

Comments: Early spring in the Appalachian Mountains moves north from week to week. Groups of Wood Anemone can be found along the roadsides in the Great Smoky Mountains National Park in late April, on the Appalachian Trail around Milam Gap, Shenandoah National Park, in early May, and on the Escarpment Trail at North Lake in the Catskill Mountains in late May.

TALL ANEMONE OR THIMBLEWEED
Anemone virginiana
Buttercup Family (Ranunculaceae)

Description: The lobed, toothed, heavily veined leaves are opposite each other on the stem of this 2–3' plant. The 1–1½" flowers have 5 greenish white, petal-like sepals.

Bloom Season: May–July

Habitat/Range: The plant is found in rocky woods and along stream banks from Maine south to Georgia and Alabama.

Comments: Found along the farm road at Dickey Ridge in Shenandoah National Park, Virginia, and the lakefront at Hills Creek State Park and Pine Creek at Colton Point State Park, Pennsylvania.

Tall Anemone or Thimbleweed

RUE ANEMONE
Anemonella thalictroides
Buttercup Family (Ranunculaceae)

Description: Three leaves, each with 3 lobes, form a whorl on the stem below the flower cluster of this 6–8" plant. The ¼–½" flowers are white or pinkish with 5–10 petal-like sepals.

Bloom Season: April–June

Habitat/Range: Found in open wooded areas from New Hampshire to Florida.

Comments: Rue Anemone was originally classified by Linneaus, the father of the botanical classification system, as an *Anemone.* It is now classified as *Anemonella,* which means "little Anemone." As late as the middle of the 20th century, the roots were cooked and eaten as "wild potatoes."

Rue Anemone

Black Cohosh or Black Snakeroot

BLACK COHOSH OR BLACK SNAKEROOT
Cimicifuga racemosa
Buttercup Family (Ranunculaceae)

Description: The leaves are divided into many groups of 3 sharply toothed and lobed leaflets. The leaves alternate on the stem of this 3–8' plant. The tiny, white flowers appear to be all stamens. The flowers form dense clusters on a long stalk.

Bloom Season: June–August

Habitat/Range: In open and wooded areas from western Massachusetts to Southern Ontario and south to Georgia and Missouri.

Comments: As summer progresses, large colonies of Black Snakeroot start blooming throughout the Central Appalachian Mountains from the Berkshires and the Catskills south. In July at the southern border of the region in Shenandoah National Park it is not unusual to see numerous plants at the edge of Skyline Drive and in the woods. Another species that looks very much like Black Snakeroot, Bugbane *(Cimicifuga americana),* grows in the mountains of Pennsylvania and West Virginia. Bugbane does not get as tall and has one small difference in the number of parts in the flower.

Virgin's Bower

VIRGIN'S BOWER
Clematis virginiana
Buttercup Family (Ranunculaceae)

Description: The leaves on this vine are divided into 3 toothed leaflets. The 1" white flowers have 4 petals. The fruit is a cluster of feathery hairs called Old Man's Beard.

Bloom Season: July–September

Habitat/Range: A long vine climbing over bushes and along streams and rivers from Nova Scotia to Georgia.

Comments: Some people develop skin rashes if they touch this plant, which grows along the creeks of north-central Pennsylvania and in Pine Grove State Park, Pennsylvania. It also is found in the Catskill Mountains of New York and the eastern boundary of the Appalachians in Maryland.

SHARP-LOBED HEPATICA
Hepatica acutiloba
Buttercup Family (Ranunculaceae)

Description: The leaves have 3 pointed lobes and are at the base of this 3–8" plant. When the flowers bloom there may be some old leaves from last year. New leaves usually start to grow as the flowers die off. The ½–1" flowers have 6–12 white, blue, or pink petal-like sepals. Several different colored flowers can grow in each group.

Bloom Season: March–May

Habitat/Range: One of the earliest blooms of spring in rich, wooded areas, often near streams, from Nova Scotia south to Florida.

Comments: Round-Lobed Hepatica or Liverleaf *(Hepatica americana)* is also one of the earliest spring plants in the Appalachian Mountains. The difference between the two plants is in the shape of their leaves as the common name indicates.

Sharp-Lobed Hepatica

GOLDENSEAL OR ORANGEROOT
Hydrastis canadensis
Buttercup Family (Ranunculaceae)

Description: The maple-shaped leaves alternate on the stem of this 8–15" plant. The ½" white flowers are composed of a tuft of stamens.

Bloom Season: May

Habit/Range: A woodland plant found from Vermont to Minnesota and south to Georgia and Arkansas.

Comments: Goldenseal is a popular folk medicine because it contains the antibacterial berberine. Unfortunately, it has become less common in some of our eastern deciduous forests because of excessive harvesting.

Goldenseal or Orangeroot

Tall Meadow Rue

TALL MEADOW RUE
Thalictrum polygamum
Buttercup Family (Ranunculaceae)

Description: The leaves have 3 pointed lobes and alternate on the stem of this 3–8' plant. The ¼–½", white, 4-petal flowers form dangling clusters.

Bloom Season: June–August

Habitat/Range: Found from Newfoundland to Florida. Its favorite habitat is a warm, sunny swamp, but it is also found along sunny spots on trails and wood roads in forests.

Comments: Tall Meadow Rue grows along Pine Creek in Pennsylvania and along the Appalachian Trail in Shenandoah National Park in Virginia. The species name of Tall Meadow Rue, *polygamum,* is applied to those plants that have 3 types of flowers: flowers that have both stamen and pistils and flowers that have only stamen or only pistils.

Waxy Meadow Rue

WAXY MEADOW RUE
Thalictrum revolutum
Buttercup Family (Ranunculaceae)

Description: Divided into lobed leaflets, the leaves alternate on the stem of this 2–6' plant. The flowers have 4 small white petals with extended, drooping stamens.

Bloom Season: May–June

Habitat/Range: On rocky, wooded slopes and sometimes in meadows from Massachusetts to Ontario and south to South Carolina and Missouri.

Comments: Early Meadow Rue *(Thalictrum dioicum)* also grows in the same habitat in the Appalachian Mountains, but it blooms about one month earlier than Waxy Meadow Rue. The plant is very similar in appearance. The flowers are greenish yellow, and the drooping stamens are smaller than those of Waxy Meadow Rue.

NEW JERSEY TEA

Ceanothus americanus
Buckthorn Family (Rhamnaceae)

Description: The ovate, toothed leaves alternate on the stem of this 1½–3' shrub. The ¼" white flowers have 5 petals and form in long clusters.

Bloom Season: June–September

Habitat/Range: Found in dry open woods and on rocky banks from Maine to Ontario and south to Florida and Texas.

Comments: New Jersey Tea grows along the trails lining the ridges of Shenandoah National Park and Blue Mountain, Virginia, and in the state parks of north central Pennsylvania.

New Jersey Tea

Mountain Shadbush or Mountain Serviceberry

MOUNTAIN SHADBUSH OR MOUNTAIN SERVICEBERRY

Amelanchier bartramiana
Rose Family (Rosaceae)

Description: The toothed, ovate leaves alternate on the stem of this 6–15' shrub. The leaves have a whitish bloom on the bottom. The ¾–1" flowers have 5 white, star-shaped petals. The flowers grow in loose bunches at the end of a branch.

Bloom Season: April–May

Habitat/Range: In moist wooded areas, swamps, and bogs from Maine to southwestern Quebec and south to Georgia.

Comments: These shrubs are also called Juneberries, because the edible fruit on many of the shadbush shrubs ripens in June. The name shadbush refers to the folklore that the shrub blooms when the shad are running. Serviceberry refers to the use of branches as altar decorations in churches at Easter. It is difficult to separate one shadbush from another when the tree is blooming because there are small distinctions between the leaves and flowers of these shrubs. It is a little easier when the fruit is ripe.

Goatsbeard

GOATSBEARD
Aruncus dioicus
Rose Family (Rosaceae)

Description: The leaves are divided into 5 ovate, toothed leaflets. The tiny flowers have 5 white petals and form a long, slender cluster on the branch of this 3–6' shrub.

Bloom Season: April–June

Habitat/Range: Leaning out over back roads and streams or erect in rich wooded areas from Pennsylvania to Iowa and south to Georgia and Missouri.

Comments: In mid-April the roads of the Southern Appalachian Mountains have sprigs of Goatsbeard leaning over the road; in June, the cliffs along Skyline Drive in Shenandoah National Park display their Goatsbeard.

COMMON STRAWBERRY OR WILD STRAWBERRY
Fragaria virginiana
Rose Family (Rosaceae)

Description: The leaves are divided into 3 toothed, ovate leaflets and are at the base of this 2–6" plant. The ½–¾" white flowers have 5 petals.

Bloom Season: March–June and sometimes October–November

Habitat/Range: In dry soils from Newfoundland to Alberta and south to Georgia and Oklahoma.

Comments: The small red fruit is edible and juicy, but it takes a lot of picking to make a pie. The genus name, *Fragaria*, means "sweet smelling."

Common Strawberry or Wild Strawberry

WHITE AVENS

Geum canadense
Rose Family (Rosaceae)

Description: The divided and toothed leaves alternate with small, undivided leaves on the stem of this 1½–3' plant. The ½" white flowers have 5 petals and a bristly disk.

Bloom Season: June–September

Habitat/Range: A very common plant along woodland trails and in woods from Nova Scotia to Georgia.

Comments: This plant—found along the trails in the parks of the Appalachian Mountains—often goes unnoticed. Many of the plants that bloom in dense, wooded areas in summertime have small, white flowers. The White Avens flower is actually larger than those of most of these plants.

White Avens

Chokecherry

CHOKECHERRY

Prunus virginiana
Rose Family (Rosaceae)

Description: This small tree or shrub is from 2–10' tall. The leaves are ovate and are sharp toothed. The small branches emit a foul odor if bruised or broken. The ¼" flowers have 5 white petals and form a dense, sweet-smelling and elongated cluster.

Bloom Season: April–June

Habitat/Range: Along wood borders and wayside thickets from Newfoundland to British Columbia and south to Maryland and northern Georgia, eastern Kentucky, Illinois, New Mexico, and California.

Comments: The fruits of this cherry range in color from dark red to purplish black and are approximately ⅜" in diameter. They are very astringent, hence the common name, Chokecherry. In June, these shrubs bloom along trails and at the edges of parking areas throughout Shenandoah National Park in Virginia. The flowers resemble those of Black Cherry (*Prunus serotina*), a tree commonly found in the Central Appalachian Mountains.

Common Blackberry

COMMON BLACKBERRY
Rubus alleghaniensis
Rose Family (Rosaceae)

Description: The divided and toothed leaves do not appear at flowering time on the 2–4' woody stems. The ½–1" white flowers have 5 petals.

Bloom Season: May–June

Habitat/Range: In dry soils from Nova Scotia to North Carolina.

Comments: Many varieties of blackberries grow in the Central Appalachian Mountains. The fruit ripens in August and September and is so plentiful that all the restaurants in Virginia's Shenandoah National Park feature blackberry ice cream. However, it is illegal to pick berries on a commercial scale in Shennandoah National Park itself. Visitors are welcome to pick enough for their personal consumption. Birds and bears love them, too.

MULTIFLORA ROSE
Rosa multiflora
Rose Family (Rosaceae)

Description: The leaves—made up of 5–7 toothed leaflets—are on the flowering stem of this 2–6' shrub. The 1–1½" flowers have 5 white petals and grow in small bunches of 3–5 flowers at the end of the stem.

Bloom Season: May–June

Habitat/Range: In moist thickets and woods and along roadsides from New England south to Florida, and it is native to Asia.

Comments: This very invasive plant can take over the entire forest floor. Woods along streams are particularly vulnerable. Multiflora Rose came to this country from Asia. At the height of the Depression in the 1930s, the United States Department of Agriculture recommended Multiflora Rose to farmers as a living fence to save both time and money. The same properties that made it a good fence, along with no natural enemies, easy self-propagation, very thorny stems, and deep taproots, also make it a pest that is hard to eradicate.

Multiflora Rose

Wine Raspberry or Wineberry

WINE RASPBERRY OR WINEBERRY
Rubus phoenicolasius
Rose Family (Rosaceae)

Description: The leaves are made up of 3 heart-shaped, toothed leaflets that have a silvery undersurface and purplish veins. The leaves alternate on the stem of this 1–4' plant. The stems of the shrub are red, bristly, and sparsely prickly. The ½" flowers have 5 small, white petals. The fruit is red.

Bloom Season: May–June

Habitat/Range: Easily spread, it escaped from cultivation into meadows, roadsides, and wooded areas. This shrub is native to eastern Asia.

Comments: This plant is invasive and often takes over a natural habitat, spreading easily because wherever its stem touches the ground it forms a new root. It is used as an ornamental because of its foliage. The berries are edible.

Canadian Burnet

CANADIAN BURNET
Sanguisorba canadensis
Rose Family (Rosaceae)

Description: The leaves—which alternate on the stem of this 1–4' plant—have 7–15 toothed, lanceolate leaflets. The tiny, white flowers form a dense spike. Each flower has 4 petals and 4 long stamens.

Bloom Season: July–October

Habitat/Range: In swamps and low meadows from Newfoundland to Michigan and south to Georgia.

Comments: Sometimes called American Burnet, it can be found in Shenandoah National Park in the area of The Big Meadow. The genus name *Sanguisorba* means "blood absorbing," and there is a red-flowered European variety that is supposed to have this property.

NARROW-LEAVED MEADOWSWEET
Spiraea alba
Rose Family (Rosaceae)

Description: The lanceolate, slightly toothed, and stalkless leaves alternate on the stem of this 2–4' plant. The small, white flowers have 5 petals and cluster to form a steeple.

Bloom Season: June–September

Habitat/Range: In wet soils from Ontario to Virginia.

Comments: Narrow-Leaved Meadowsweet can be found as far south as the Central Appalachian Mountains of Virginia. The narrow leaves and the brown bark distinguish this meadowsweet from *Spiraea latifolia,* which can have either pink or white flowers but does not grow in the southern end of the Central Appalachian Mountains.

Narrow-Leaved Meadowsweet

MEADOWSWEET
Spiraea latifolia
Rose Family (Rosaceae)

Description: The toothed, ovate leaves alternate on the reddish or purple stem of this 2–6' shrub. The ⅙–¼" white or pale pink, 5-petal flowers form a cone-shaped cluster.

Bloom Season: June–September

Habitat/Range: In moist or rocky ground from Newfoundland to Saskatchewan and south to Pennsylvania.

Comments: Some plant-growth boundaries are very distinct. This shrub is a good example. It is found as far south as the mountains of Pennsylvania, but more commonly in the Appalachian Mountains of New England and in the Adirondack Mountains of New York.

Meadowsweet

Miterwort or Bishop's Cap

MITERWORT OR BISHOP'S CAP
Mitella diphylla
Saxifrage Family (Saxifragaceae)

Description: The lobed and toothed, heart-shaped leaves grow from the base of this 6–16" plant. The ¼" flowers have 5 petals that form a tiny, white, fringed bell.

Bloom Season: March–June

Habitat/Range: In rich woods from Quebec to Minnesota and south to North Carolina and Missouri.

Comments: This plant is also called Fairy-cup because of its very pretty fringed flowers. It is the type of flower whose beauty is best appreciated through a magnifying glass.

Foamflower or False Miterwort

FOAMFLOWER OR FALSE MITERWORT
Tiarella cordifolia
Saxifrage Family (Saxifragaceae)

Description: The lobed and toothed leaves grow from the base of this 6–12" plant. The ½" flowers have 5 white petals. The flowers grow on the top portion of the plant's stem, forming a small pyramid.

Bloom Season: April–June

Habitat/Range: In rich, moist woods from Nova Scotia to Minnesota and south to eastern Alabama and western Georgia, especially in the mountains.

Comments: Foamflower blooms for a few weeks in Fort Mountain State Park in Georgia beginning in mid-April. In New Hampshire's White Mountains, it blooms in late June. Tiarella means "little tiara," which was the headdress of the ancient Persians.

WHITE TURTLEHEAD
Chelone glabra
Snapdragon Family (Scrophulariaceae)

Description: The toothed, lanceolate leaves are opposite each other on the stem of this 1–3' plant. The petals of the 1–1½" white flowers form a lipped tube.

Bloom Season: July–September

Habitat/Range: In moist grounds along streams and lakefronts from Newfoundland to Minnesota and south to Georgia and Mississippi.

Comments: The egg-shaped tube that makes up the flower is often parted into 2 open lips at the end, similar to the shape of a turtle's head, although some think it resembles a snake's head because in some areas it is called Snakehead. The Southern Appalachian Mountains are home to a pink variety *(Chelone obliqua)*.

White Turtlehead

FOXGLOVE BEARDTONGUE OR WHITE BEARDTONGUE
Penstemon digitalis
Snapdragon Family (Scrophulariaceae)

Description: The lanceolate, toothed, stalk-less leaves grow opposite each other on the stem of this 2–4' plant. The 1½–2", white or purple-tinged flowers have 5 petals and are trumpet shaped and swollen in the middle. The flowers form a cluster at the top of the plant.

Bloom Season: June–August

Habitat/Range: In fields and thickets from Maine to Tennessee and from Illinois and Kansas to Arkansas.

Comments: Foxglove Beardtongue grows in Colton State Park and Hills Creek State Park in Pennsylvania in July as well as at Shenandoah National Park in Virginia in June.

Foxglove Beardtongue or White Beardtongue

Horse Nettle

HORSE NETTLE
Solanum carolinense
Potato Family (Solanaceae)

Description: The lobed and toothed leaves alternate on the stem of this 1–4' plant. The leaves have prickles on the lower sides along the mid-rib. The 1–1½", star-shaped flowers have 5 purple or white petals, and prominent yellow stamens form a cone in the center.

Bloom Season: May–October

Habitat/Range: In open areas from New England to Washington and south to Florida and Texas.

Comments: Despite its eye-catching flowers, Horse Nettle is considered a pest because of the prickles on its stems and leaves. The plant is more common in the southern end of the Central Appalachian Mountains.

Honewort

HONEWORT
Cryptotaenia canadensis
Parsley Family (Umbelliferae)

Description: The leaves alternate on the stem of this 1–3' plant and are divided into 3 toothed and often lobed parts. The tiny flowers have 5 white petals and form several small clusters.

Bloom Season: June–September

Habitat/Range: In woods from New Brunswick to South Dakota and south to Florida and Texas.

Comments: Honewort is one of very few plants that bloom in shaded summer woods. The tiny, white flowers form small clusters, so it easily goes unnoticed by people on trails. It is a very common plant in the summer woods of a large region of the United States.

QUEEN ANNE'S LACE OR WILD CARROT
Daucus carota
Parsley Family (Umbelliferae)

Description: The finely divided leaves alternate on the stem of this 2–3' plant. The tiny flowers have 5 white petals, and there is often 1 dark purple or black center flower in the 4–6" umbel the white flowers form. There are rare groups of Queen Anne's Lace with pink flowers.

Bloom Season: May–October

Habitat/Range: On roadsides and in open places throughout North America.

Comments: Originating in Europe, this beautiful plant is a pest in some parts of North America because it propagates so easily and takes over entire areas. The edible carrot is the root of an Asian relative of this plant. The root of Queen Anne's Lace is white.

Queen Anne's Lace or Wild Carrot

COW PARSNIP
Heracleum maximum
Parsley Family (Umbelliferae)

Description: The large maplelike leaves alternate and clasp the stem of this 3–6' plant. The tiny, 5-petal, white flowers form a large, flat cluster.

Bloom Season: June–August

Habitat/Range: In moist and rich soils from Newfoundland to Alaska and south to Florida and California.

Comments: Native Americans used a tea made from the root of this plant to cure a variety of complaints. The foliage is poisonous to livestock and the sap can cause skin irritations.

Cow Parsnip

Aniseroot or Long-Styles Sweet Cicely

ANISEROOT OR LONG-STYLES SWEET CICELY
Osmorhiza longistylis
Parsley Family (Umbelliferae)

Description: The fernlike leaves alternate on the stem of this 1–3' woodland plant. The ⅛" flowers are white, have 5 petals, and form small umbels. The styles of the flower protrude beyond the petals.

Bloom Season: March through June

Habitat/Range: In wooded areas throughout the eastern United States.

Comments: The root of this plant has the shape of a carrot and smells like licorice. Native Americans used the plant medicinally. A good spot to look for it is the northern part of Shenandoah National Park in the Dickey Ridge area.

Cowbane

COWBANE
Oxypolis rigidior
Parsley Family (Umbelliferae)

Description: The leaves are divided into opposite, sparsely toothed, narrow, lanceolate leaflets. The leaves alternate on the stem of this 2–6' plant. The tiny, 5-petal, white flowers form flat clusters.

Bloom Season: August–September

Habitat/Range: In swamps and wet woods from New York to Minnesota and south to Florida and Texas.

Comments: This plant is poisonous, as are many plants with 5-petal, white flowers that form a flat cluster in the parsley family (Umbelliferae). It is best to be wary of using any part of these plants for any purpose except decoration.

WHITE VERVAIN
Verbena urticifolia
Vervain Family (Verbenaceae)

Description: The toothed, lanceolate leaves are opposite each other on the stem of this 2–5' plant. The tiny, white flowers form an interrupted spike.

Bloom Season: June–September

Habitat/Range: In fields from New Brunswick to South Dakota and south to Texas and Florida.

Comments: The English name of this plant seems to be an Anglicized version of the Latin word *verbena*. In classical Rome a verbena was a sacred herb or branch carried in ceremonies.

White Vervain

CANADA VIOLET

Viola canadensis
Violet Family (Violacaea)

Description: The toothed, heart-shaped leaves alternate on the stem of this 4–8" plant. The ½–1" white flowers have a yellow throat. Each flower has 5 petals.

Bloom Season: March through May and sometimes October through November

Habitat/Range: In mountains and wooded uplands from Newfoundland to eastern British Columbia, in the Rockies, and south to Arizona, New Mexico, and Alabama.

Comments: Another white violet that is commonly found in the Central Appalachian Mountains is Northern White Violet *(Viola pallens)*. Canada Violet is one of the violets that can be tricked by warm weather in October and November to bloom for a second time in the year.

Canada Violet

FIELD PANSY

Viola kitaibeliana
Violet Family (Violacaea)

Description: The spoon-shaped leaves are opposite each other on the stem of this 4–6" plant. The ½–¾" white flower has 5 petals, each with thin purple stripes radiating from a bright yellow center.

Bloom Season: April–May

Habitat/Range: Along roads and in meadows from New York to Iowa and south to Georgia and Texas.

Comments: This delicate little violet is often overlooked because of its size and muted colors. It grows in large groups and is quite pretty.

Field Pansy

YELLOW FLOWERS

Spatterdock Pond Lily

Yellow Stargrass

YELLOW STARGRASS
Hypoxis hirsuta
Amaryllis Family (Amaryllidaceae)

Description: The grasslike leaves are at the base of this 3–6" plant. The ½–¾" yellow flowers form a star.

Bloom Season: April–September

Habitat/Range: In dry soils in meadows and open woods from Maine to Manitoba and south to Florida and Texas.

Comments: Clusters of these flowers and their bright yellow stars light up a woodland glen, as in Catoctin Mountains Park, Maryland, the home of the presidential retreat, Camp David.

SKUNK CABBAGE
Symplocarpus foetidus
Arum Family (Araceae)

Description: The very large, egg-shaped leaves are a familiar sight in wet places, but there are none at flowering time on this 12–18" plant. The 6–8" red, often mottled hood (spathe) surrounds a knob-shaped cluster of yellow flowers (spadix).

Bloom Season: January–May

Habitat/Range: In wet and swampy places from Nova Scotia to Minnesota and south to North Carolina and Iowa.

Comments: When Skunk Cabbage starts blooming in January and February—sometimes pushing up through snow and ice—it often goes unnoticed. Instead, what is noticed in swampy areas are the huge leaves that give this plant its name. When a leaf is broken, it emits a foul odor.

Skunk Cabbage

PALE JEWELWEED OR PALE TOUCH-ME-NOT

Impatiens pallida
Jewelweed Family (Balsaminaceae)

Description: The egg-shaped, slightly toothed leaves alternate on the stem of this 1–5' plant. The 1–2" flowers are yellow, and the petals form a tilted cup with a lip.

Bloom Season: June–September

Habitat/Range: In damp woods and thickets, particularly near streams, from Quebec to Saskatchewan and south to North Carolina, Tennessee, and Missouri.

Comments: Less common than Orange Jewelweed *(Impatiens capensis),* it can be found in large quantities in many locations in the Central Appalachian Mountains. It grows both on Blue Mountain and in Shenandoah National Park in Virginia and along both banks of Pine Creek Gorge in Pennsylvania.

Pale Jewelweed or Pale Touch-Me-Not

Tower Mustard

TOWER MUSTARD

Arabis glabra
Mustard Family (Brassicaceae)

Description: The clasping, lanceolate, downy leaves alternate on the stem of this 1–4' plant. The ¼" flowers have 4 cream-white or yellow petals and form a domed cluster.

Bloom Season: May–July

Habitat/Range: In fields, open areas, and rocky places from Quebec to Alaska and southward to North Carolina, Arkansas, New Mexico, and California.

Comments: All mustards have 4 petals and most have yellow petals. Some mustard plants will cover a fallow field, producing a patch of golden yellow on the landscape. Tower Mustard tends to be a solitary plant growing in small groups in rocky places and along abandoned rail beds. Tower Mustard belongs to a group that is also called Sicklepods. These plants produce pods that are almost 4" long with seeds so tiny that the pod is only ¹⁄₂₅" thick.

Early Winter Cress

EARLY WINTER CRESS
Barbarea verna
Mustard Family (Brassicaceae)

Description: The leaves at the base of the plant have 8–20 lobes, and the terminal lobe is round. The stem leaves alternate on this 1–2' plant. The ¼–½" flowers have 4 yellow petals. The flowers form small clusters.

Bloom Season: March–May

Habitat/Range: In open places from Massachusetts to Southern New York; also in the Southern Appalachian Mountains and on the West Coast.

Comment: Cultivated in some areas as a salad green. The mature pods can be up to 3" long.

COMMON WINTER CRESS OR YELLOW ROCKET
Barbarea vulgaris
Mustard Family (Brassicaceae)

Common Winter Cress or Yellow Rocket

Description: The leaves at the base of the plant have 2–8 lobes, with an ovate terminal lobe. The stem leaves are toothed and alternate. The plant is 1–2' tall. The ¼" flowers have 4 yellow petals. The flowers form small clusters.

Bloom Season: April–August

Habitat/Range: In fields and open places from Labrador to southern Virginia; also on the West Coast and in the Great Smoky Mountains.

Comments: This plant and Early Winter Cress *(Barbarea verna)* are similar in appearance, with a few things that distinguish one from the other. The base leaves look different when examined side by side. The generally smaller Common Winter Cress flowers bloom in late spring and continue to bloom all summer. While Early Winter Cress gets a head start in spring, it then stops flowering when the weather gets warm.

Treacle Mustard or Wormseed

TREACLE MUSTARD OR WORMSEED
Erysimum cheiranthoides
Mustard Family (Brassicaceae)

Description: The entire, lanceolate leaves alternate on the stem of this 1–4' plant. The ¼" yellow flowers have 4 petals and form a small cluster at the end of the stem.

Bloom Season: June–September

Habitat/Range: Along streams and fields from Newfoundland to Pennsylvania.

Comments: There are many yellow mustard plants, and a few are grown commercially. This mustard also appears in northern Europe, on the Pacific Coast, and in the Central Appalachian Mountains along Pine Creek in Pennsylvania.

Wild Radish or Jointed Charlock

WILD RADISH OR JOINTED CHARLOCK
Raphanus raphnistrum
Mustard Family (Brassicaceae)

Description: The deeply divided leaves are at the base of this 6–18" plant. As the leaves ascend the stem they get smaller. The lower ones can be up to 8" long. The ½–¾", light yellow, 4-petal flowers fade to white as they age.

Bloom Season: June–October

Habitat/Range: In fields and along railroad tracks and old railroad beds almost everywhere in the United States and Canada.

Comments: The flowers on the radish *(Raphanus sativas)* grown in gardens and eaten in salads are purple. The cultivated radish plant has escaped from gardens and is occasionally found in the Central Appalachian Mountains. The Wild Radish is native to Europe, and many consider it a weed.

NODDING BUR MARIGOLD
Bidens cernua
Composite Family (Compositae)

Description: The toothed, long, narrow, lanceolate leaves are opposite each other on the stem of this 1–6' tall plant. The 1–1 ½" yellow flowers have 6–8 often reflexed petals surrounding a disk.

Bloom Season: August–October

Habitat/Range: From Nova Scotia to Hudson Bay and British Columbia and south to North Carolina. Also found in California.

Comments: *Bidens*—found in Hills Creek State Park in Pennsylvania—are also called Beggar Ticks. They get their name because the seeds they produce adhere to the surface of anything that brushes against them. The seed covers have 2 sharp barbs that stick to hikers' clothing like ticks. This is the way these plants spread their seeds and propagate in new locations.

Nodding Bur Marigold

BEGGAR TICKS OR STICKTIGHT
Bidens fronsdosa
Composite Family (Compositae)

Description: The divided, toothed leaves are opposite on the stem of this 1–4' plant. The ½" flower heads have greenish yellow bracts that look like petals.

Bloom Season: September

Habitat/Range: In wet and dry soils from Nova Scotia to Florida and British Colombia to California and Colorado.

Comments: The name comes from the seed that sticks to clothing or fur. This is the way these plants spread their seeds and propagate in new locations. Beggar Ticks can be found in both Bear Mountain and Harriman State Parks in New York.

Beggar Ticks or Sticktight

Lance-Leaved Coreopsis

LANCE-LEAVED COREOPSIS
Coreopsis lanceolata
Composite Family (Compositae)

Description: There is a lanceolate base leaf with 1 lobe and lanceolate stem leaves that are opposite each other on the stem of this 1–2' plant. The 1½–2½" flowers have 6–10 yellow petals. The petals have several notches.

Bloom Season: May–July

Habitat/Range: Having escaped from gardens, this plant can be found in any part of the Central Appalachian Mountains that is now or was once inhabited and on the Piedmont and Coastal Plain of the central Atlantic states.

Comments: Shenandoah National Park was private land until the 1930s when the farmers' and residents' land was purchased by the Commonwealth of Virginia, and the residents were relocated to the valleys in the area. Lance-Leaved Coreopsis grows at several locations in the park.

Sneezeweed

SNEEZEWEED
Helenium autumnale
Composite Family (Compositae)

Description: The stem leaves are toothed and extend down the stem, forming wings. The leaves alternate on the stem of this 2–6' plant. The 1–2" yellow flowers have wedge–shaped petals, and the center disk is yellow and knob shaped.

Bloom Season: July–October

Habitat/Range: In moist soils practically throughout the United States and southern Canada.

Comments: Sneezeweeds get their name from a practice of Native Americans who sniffed a powder made of dried, nearly mature flower heads as a cure for colds. Sneezeweed is found in the Pine Creek stream valley in Pennsylvania.

PURPLE-HEADED SNEEZEWEED
Helenium nudiflorum
Composite Family (Compositae)

Description: The stem leaves are entire or have a few teeth and extend down the stem, forming wings. The leaves alternate on the stem of this 1–3' plant. The 1–1½" flowers have wedge-shaped yellow petals and a brown or purple knob-shaped disk.

Bloom Season: July–October

Habitat/Range: In open places and on roadsides, a native of the southern United States introduced into the northern states.

Comments: It also can be found along Pine Creek in Pennsylvania. Both *Helenium autumnale* and *nudiflorum* are grown at Bowman's Hill Wildflower Preserve, an outdoor Pennsylvania native plant museum in Bucks County, Pennsylvania.

Purple-Headed Sneezeweed

Common Sunflower

COMMON SUNFLOWER
Helianthus annuus
Composite Family (Compositae)

Description: The heart-shaped, rough, toothed leaves are placed singly on the stem of this 3–12' plant. The 3–5" yellow flowers have a brown disk.

Bloom Season: July–October

Habitat/Range: Found in open places and native to states from Minnesota to Idaho and south to Texas and California. Quite common in the northeastern states and found in river valleys and along roads in the Appalachian Mountains.

Comments: The flowers of the wild Common Sunflower are often less than half the size of the cultivated plant. The flowers yield a golden dye and the edible seeds are pressed to obtain a useful cooking oil. The plants in the Appalachian Mountains might be the offspring of cultivated plants that have found their way back to the wild.

Thin-Leaved Sunflower

THIN-LEAVED SUNFLOWER
Helianthus decapetalus
Composite Family (Compositae)

Description: The toothed leaves are thin and the upper leaves are usually alternate, with the lower leaves opposite each other on the stem of this 2–5' plant. The 2–3" yellow flowers have a yellow disk and usually have 10 petals.

Bloom Season: July–September

Habitat/Range: In moist woods and along streams from Quebec to Michigan and south to Georgia, Tennessee, and Missouri.

Comments: There are about 70 species of sunflowers native to the New World and this is one of several varieties commonly found in the Appalachian Mountains. Early in July, Skyline Drive in Shenandoah National Park, Virginia, is lined with wonderful displays of bright sunflowers and Thin-Leaved is among the ones seen on moist wooded banks.

WOODLAND SUNFLOWER
Helianthus divaricatus
Composite Family (Compositae)

Description: The lanceolate, toothed leaves have a very short stalk and are opposite each other on the stem of this 2–5' plant. The leaves have a rounded, broad base and one main vein. The 2–4" flowers have 8–12 yellow petals and a yellow disk. The disk is about ½".

Bloom Season: July–September

Habitat/Range: In moist woods and along streams from Pennsylvania to Georgia and west to Ohio, Missouri, and Louisiana.

Comments: The Small-Woodland Sunflower *(Helianthus microcephalus)* looks a good deal like its larger relative the Woodland Sunflower. The flowers of Small-Woodland Sunflower can be as small as 1" wide, with a ¼" disk. Often there are 2 flowers on the stem of the Small-Woodland Sunflower and the leaves are tapered on both ends.

Woodland Sunflower

PALE-LEAVED SUNFLOWER
Helianthus strumosus
Composite Family (Compositae)

Description: The toothed, lanceolate leaves are opposite each other on the stem of this 3–8' plant. The 2" flowers have 6–12 yellow petals and a yellow disk. The disk is less than 1" across.

Bloom Season: July–September

Habitat/Range: In dry woodlands and on banks from Maine south to Georgia and Arkansas.

Comments: Most sunflowers in the Central Appalachian Mountains have a much larger center disk than Pale-Leaved Sunflower. The exception is Small-Woodland Sunflower *(Helianthus microcephalus)*.

Pale-Leaved Sunflower

Oxeye

OXEYE
Heliopsis helianthoides
Composite Family (Compositae)

Description: The toothed and spatula-shaped leaves have stalks and are opposite each other on the stem of this 2–6' plant. The 2–4" yellow flowers have 10–15 petals and a yellow disk.

Bloom Season: June–October

Habitat/Range: In open places and woods from Quebec to British Columbia and south to Georgia and New Mexico.

Comments: Oxeye looks very much like a sunflower, as the botanical name indicates. *(Helianthoides* means sunflower.) The characteristic that distinguishes this genus from sunflowers is the disk of this plant and its conical shape.

Canada Hawkweed

CANADA HAWKWEED
Hieracium canadense
Composite Family (Compositae)

Description: The lanceolate, toothed leaves alternate and clasp the stem of this 1–4' plant. The 1–1½" yellow flowers look something like a dandelion.

Bloom Season: July–September

Habitat/Range: In dry woods from Newfoundland to Ontario and south to New Jersey and in British Columbia and Oregon.

Comments: Another northern species of hawkweed *(Hieracium vulgatum)* might be more easily mistaken for a dandelion than Canada Hawkweed, as its leaves are all at the base and its flower heads are larger and denser.

KING DEVIL HAWKWEED OR FIELD HAWKWEED
Hieracium pratense
Composite Family (Compositae)

Description: The lanceolate, hairy leaves have some teeth and are at the base of this 1–2' plant. The stem is also hairy. The 1½", yellow, dandelionlike flowers grow in groups at the top of the plant.

Bloom Season: May–September

Habitat/Range: In meadows and by roadsides from Quebec and Ontario south to Georgia.

Comments: This is a hawkweed that has been naturalized in eastern North America from Europe, but eastern North America also has several different kinds of native hawkweeds, may of which are illustrated in this book. This genus in Europe includes an enormous number of forms.

King Devil Hawkweed or Field Hawkweed

RATTLESNAKE WEED OR POOR ROBIN'S PLANTAIN

Hieracium venosum
Composite Family (Compositae)

Description: The lanceolate leaves have red or purple veins and grow from the base of this 6–36" plant. The ½–¾" flowers are yellow. Each flower has many square-edged petals.

Bloom Season: May–October

Habitat/Range: In open woods from Maine to Michigan and south to Florida and Louisiana.

Comments: Rattlesnake Weed is one of the dozen or more hawkweeds that grow in the eastern United States. The red- or purple-veined leaves of this hawkweed give the plant its name and make the plant unique. The veins usually fade as the plant matures. Rattlesnake Weed likes to grow where trails open up woodlands to sunlight and can best be spotted and photographed in the spring.

Rattlesnake Weed or Poor Robin's Plantain

Pineapple Weed

PINEAPPLE WEED

Matricaria matricarioides
Composite Family (Compositae)

Description: The finely divided, fernlike leaves alternate on the stem of this 6–16" plant. The ¼" yellow flowers form heads.

Bloom Season: May–October

Habitat/Range: Along roadsides, railroad tracks, and in fields. This plant is native to the western United States, but also grows east of the Mississippi River.

Comments: Sometimes trucks, cars, and trains transfer seeds of non-native plants in their undercarriages or their tires. Pineapple Weed probably was transferred from the West to the Central Appalachian Mountains this way.

Black-Eyed Susan

BLACK-EYED SUSAN
Rudbeckia hirta
Composite Family (Compositae)

Description: The lanceolate, slightly toothed, hairy, and thick leaves alternate on the stem of this 1–3' plant. The 2–4" flowers have many yellow petals and a dark brown center disk.

Bloom Season: June–September

Habitat/Range: In meadows and on prairies, widely distributed in the eastern United States and in Canada from Quebec to Manitoba.

Comments: In the Central Appalachian Mountains, large groups of large Black-Eyed Susan can usually be found on edges of roads that run along ridges and over mountains. This eye-catching flower has been named the state flower of Maryland, where the eastern edge of one portion of the Central Appalachian Mountains terminates.

GREEN-HEADED CONEFLOWER OR TALL CONEFLOWER
Rudbeckia laciniata
Composite Family (Compositae)

Description: The lower leaves are divided into toothed and lobed leaflets. The leaves alternate on the stem of this 3–10' plant. The 3–4" flowers have 6–10 downward turning, petal-like rays and a greenish yellow disk.

Bloom Season: July–September

Habitat/Range: In wet places from Quebec to Montana and south to Florida.

Comments: These coneflowers like places beside streams and lakes. They can be found near the stream in Pine Grove Furnace State Park in southern Pennsylvania and near the lake at Hills Creek State Park in northern Pennsylvania.

Green-Headed Coneflower or Tall Coneflower

GOLDEN RAGWORT
Senecio aureus
Composite Family (Compositae)

Description: The stem leaves are finely divided and there is 1 heart-shaped leaf at the base of this 6–24" plant. The ½" flowers have 8–13 yellow petals, and the disk is yellow.

Bloom Season: April–July

Habitat/Range: In wet soils from Newfoundland to Florida.

Comments: Spring flowers found in woods and along trails are often in pastel colors or white and the plants are low to the ground. Golden Ragwort stands out because it is a warm golden yellow and is usually at least 12" high when it blooms. It often grows along the trailsides, running along streams or beneath wet cliffs, or at the bottom of drainage areas.

Golden Ragwort

Slender Goldenrod

SLENDER GOLDENROD
Solidago erecta
Composite Family (Compositae)

Description: The lanceolate leaves alternate on the stem of this 2–3' plant. The ¼" flowers have 8–12 yellow petals and form a flat cluster.

Bloom Season: August–October

Habitat/Range: In dry woods from southeastern New York to Pennsylvania and south to Kentucky and Georgia.

Comments: Many types of goldenrod grow in the Appalachian Mountains, and the flowers are usually yellow (for the exception, see Silverrod). The flowers can be in the axil of the leaves, like the Blue-Stemmed Goldenrod *(Solidago caesia),* or form clusters in 1 of 3 basic shapes. The flowers can form a clublike cluster, as with the illustrated Slender Goldenrod; they can have several branching clusters, as with the Early Goldenrod *(Solidago juncea);* or they can have clusters that form a group that is flat across the top, as the Slender-leaved Goldenrod or Slender Fragrant Goldenrod *(Solidago tenuifolia).*

Early Goldenrod

EARLY GOLDENROD
Solidago juncea
Composite Family (Compositae)

Description: The almost entire leaves alternate on the stem of this 1–3' plant. The leaves and stem are smooth. The ¼–½" yellow flowers form an elm-branched cluster.

Bloom Season: July–September

Habitat/Range: In dry, open places from Nova Scotia to Saskatchewan and south to Georgia and Missouri.

Comments: Goldenrod flowers form 1 of 3 basic cluster forms. Early Goldenrod are among those goldenrods that form an elm-branched cluster and are true to their name as one of the earliest bloomers in July. Goldenrods hybridize, and the species are difficult to identify without a lot of specialized botanical knowledge.

LARGE-LEAVED GOLDENROD
Solidago macrophylla
Composite Family (Compositae)

Description: The toothed, tapered, lanceolate, 5" wide to 9" long leaves alternate on the stem of this 8–24" plant. Base leaves grow on long stalks with sharp teeth. The ¼" flowers have 8–10 yellow petals and form a clublike terminal cluster.

Bloom Season: Late August–October

Habitat/Range: From Newfoundland south to New Hampshire and New York and at high elevations in the mountains to northern Virginia.

Comments: The arrangement of flowers described here fits many goldenrods that grow in the Appalachian Mountains. It is often difficult to distinguish one goldenrod from another, but the large leaves of this goldenrod make a positive identification almost certain.

Large-Leaved Goldenrod

SPINY-LEAVED SOW-THISTLE
Sonchus asper
Composite Family (Compositae)

Description: The clasping, lobed leaves have spiny edges and alternate on the stem of this 1–5' plant. The 1–1½" yellow flowers look something like a dandelion.

Bloom Season: June–October

Habitat/Range: In dry and waste places throughout the Western Hemisphere and in northern Africa. Naturalized from Europe.

Comments: Not the prettiest of plants, the Spiny-Leaved Sow-Thistle is often large and easily noticed because of its prickly looking leaves and yellow flowers.

Spiny-Leaved Sow-Thistle

TANSY
Tanacetum vulgare
Composite Family (Compositae)

Description: The finely divided, fernlike leaves alternate on the stem of this 1–4' plant. The ½" yellow flowers have no petals and form flat clusters.

Bloom Season: July–September

Habitat/Range: Along roadsides and in open places in river valleys from Nova Scotia to Oregon and south to North Carolina, Missouri, and Nevada. Native to Europe.

Comments: At every flood time, streams and rivers spread the seeds of plants like Tansy, which colonists brought to North America. Tansy can be found at many locations along Pine Creek in Pennsylvania.

Tansy

Yellow Goat's Beard or Salsify

YELLOW GOAT'S BEARD OR SALSIFY

Tragopogon pratensis
Composite Family (Compositae)

Description: The grasslike leaves alternate on the stem of this 1–3' plant. The 1½–2½" flowers have many light yellow petals. The seeds form into a very large, round gossamer ball.

Bloom Season: May–August

Habitat/Range: In fields and open places throughout most of North America, except the southeastern states.

Comments: Yellow Goat's Beard is native to England where it is called Jack-Go-to-Bed-at-Noon because it closes at midday. The seed head of this plant is what most people notice because of its beauty and size.

Coltsfoot

COLTSFOOT
Tussilago farfara
Composite Family (Compositae)

Description: The lobed leaves have the shape of a colt's foot but are absent when this 6–18" plant blooms. The 1–2" flowers have many yellow, squared petals. The seed ball is not as feathery as a dandelion seed ball.

Bloom Season: March–May

Habitat/Range: In moist soils on banks and roadsides from Nova Scotia to southwestern Virginia.

Comments: In the southern part of its range where this plant often blooms for more than a month and grows in large patches, it is not uncommon to see the leaves, the flower, and the seed ball in one group of plants. In the northern Central Appalachian Mountains, it is rare to see any leaves before the flowers and seeds have completely disappeared.

Wingstem

WINGSTEM
Verbesina alternifolia
Composite Family (Compositae)

Description: The toothed leaves alternate on the stem of this 3–8' plant. The 1–2" yellow flowers have 10 or fewer petals and a yellow disk.

Bloom Season: August–September

Habitat/Range: In rich soils from New Jersey to Iowa and south to Kansas and Florida.

Comments: Found along the Appalachian Trail in Michaux Forest and at other lower elevations in central and southern Pennsylvania. Wingstems like the rich moist soils found near streams and rivers that overflow their banks.

SPICEBUSH
Lindera benzoin
Heath Family (Ericaceae)

Description: There are no leaves on this 3–15' shrub when it flowers. The ¼" fragrant, yellow flowers form small tufts along the bare branch. When the flowers die, the leaves that emerge are ovate and alternate on the branch of the shrub.

Bloom Season: March–May

Habitat/Range: In moist wooded areas and thickets and along streams from Maine and New Hampshire to Michigan and south to North Carolina and Kansas.

Comments: This is one of the first bushes to bloom in the spring. In the Appalachian Mountains it is often found on trails and roadsides that run along streams. There is a spicy aroma in wooded areas where there are many Spicebush in bloom.

Spicebush

Birdsfoot Trefoil

BIRDSFOOT TREFOIL
Lotus corniculatus
Pea Family (Fabaceae)

Description: The leaves are divided into 5 rounded leaflets. The leaves alternate on the stem of this 4–8" plant. The 1" flowers are bright yellow and pealike.

Bloom Season: June–September

Habitat/Range: In meadows and open places from Nova Scotia to Maryland.

Comments: Birdsfoot Trefoil comes back each year from a long root. It is found throughout the Central Appalachian Mountains. Large groups grow near the lake at Hills Creek State Park, Pennsylvania, and Lake Kanawaki, Harriman State Park, New York.

Coppery St. Johnswort

COPPERY ST. JOHNSWORT
Hypericum denticulatum
St. Johnswort Family (Guiterrae)

Description: The ovate leaves are stalkless and bend upward and opposite each other on the stem of this 8–20" plant. The ½–¾", coppery yellow, 5-petal flowers have a small notch or dent *(denticulatum)* at the end of the petal.

Bloom Season: July–September

Habitat/Range: In moist soils from New York to Pennsylvania and south to Florida.

Comments: Some botanists consider Coppery St. Johnswort a southeastern plant. However, it grows in northern Pennsylvania and in the Catskills.

COMMON ST. JOHNSWORT
Hypericum perforatum
St. Johnswort Family (Guiterrae)

Description: The thin, ovate, entire leaves are opposite each other on the stem of this 12–24" branched plant. The ½" flowers have 5 yellow petals with small black dots at the edge of the petals. The stamens are united in groups of 3 and raised in a prominent center grouping.

Bloom Season: June–September

Habitat/Range: Native to Europe, this common plant of fields and waste places now grows throughout the United States.

Comments: The plant is used commercially to produce over-the-counter medications for controlling depression.

Common St. Johnswort

WITCH HAZEL
Hamamelis virginia
Witch Hazel Family (Hamamelidaceae)

Description: The wavy-toothed, ovate leaves of this 5–15' shrub or small tree have mostly turned their autumn yellow at flowering time. The 1" flowers have 4 narrow yellow petals.

Bloom Season: September–October in the north and December–February in Florida and Texas.

Habitat/Range: In woods from Nova Scotia to Ontario and south to Florida and Texas.

Comments: Witch hazel, an astringent, is made from this plant. A large grove of these shrubs can be found blooming in October off the Hog Rock Nature Trail in Catoctin National Park, Maryland.

Witch Hazel

Yellow Iris

YELLOW IRIS
Iris pseudacorus
Iris Family (Iridaceae)

Description: The grasslike, 1–2" wide leaves alternate on the stem of this 1–3' plant. The 4" flowers have 3 yellow petals.

Bloom Season: April–July

Habitat/Range: In wet places by lakes and streams and in marshes from Massachusetts to southern New Jersey and at low elevations in the Great Smoky Mountains of Tennessee and North Carolina.

Comments: Yellow Iris escaped from cultivation and is found throughout the Appalachian Mountains. The lakefront at Hills Creek State Park in Pennsylvania has several stands of Yellow Irises. There are also native irises that grow in the Appalachian Mountains. The most common of these is the familiar purple Larger Blueflag Iris *(Iris versicolor),* found east of the Appalachians.

Yellow Clintonia or Corn-Lily

YELLOW CLINTONIA OR CORN-LILY

Clintonia borealis
Lily Family (Lilliaceae)

Description: The large, broad, and shiny entire leaves are at the base of this 6–12" plant. The ¾", bell-shaped flowers have 6 yellow petals with a greenish cast.

Bloom Season: May–August

Habitat/Range: In moist, rocky wooded areas and high meadows from Labrador to Manitoba and south to New England, Wisconsin, and south in the mountains to Georgia.

Comments: The flowers last a very short time and what is most noticeable in the woods is the bright blue berry that this plant produces in the fall. This is reflected in other common names of the plant: Blue Bead and Dog Berry. The plant blooms in May in the south and as late as August in the far north and at high altitudes.

Yellow Adder's Tongue or Yellow Trout Lily

YELLOW ADDER'S TONGUE OR YELLOW TROUT LILY

Erythronium americanum
Lily Family (Lilliaceae)

Description: The 4–8" entire, lanceolate leaves are at the base of this 3–6" plant. The smooth leaves have a mottled appearance when they first appear. The 1–2" flowers have 6 yellow, bell-shaped, and reflexed petals and bright red stamens.

Bloom Season: March–May

Habitat/Range: In moist, rich wooded areas and thickets from Nova Scotia to Minnesota and south to Florida.

Comments: The plant can be found throughout the Central Appalachian range. The Iroquois used the plant medicinally. The roots were used to control fevers, and the leaves were used to heal skin ulcers. This plant is also called Dog Tooth Violet.

Sessile Bellwort or Wild Oats

SESSILE BELLWORT OR WILD OATS

Uvularia sessilifolia
Lily Family (Lilliaceae)

Description: The lanceolate, smooth leaves alternate on the stem of this 6–10" plant. The ½–¾" bell-shaped flowers have 6 pale yellow petals.

Bloom Season: May–June

Habitat/Range: Common in wooded areas and thickets from New Brunswick to Minnesota and south to Georgia and Arkansas.

Comments: Found on the Escarpment Trail in the North Lake region of the Catskill Mountains. In the 18th century, the young shoots of this plant were considered a delicacy, tasting like asparagus. However tempting it is to revive this practice, please remember that plants in state or national parks and forests cannot be disturbed.

SPATTERDOCK POND LILY OR COW LILY

Nuphar variegatum
Water Lily Family (Nymphaeaceae)

Description: The heart-shaped leaves are at the base of this plant. The 2–3" flowers have 5 or 6 yellow sepals that look like petals and form a globe open at the top.

Bloom Season: June–October

Habitat/Range: In swamps, ponds, and streams across Canada and south to Maryland, Iowa, and Montana.

Comments: This is also called Bullhead Lily because the sepals are often red on the inner side.

JANET MEDINA

Spatterdock Pond Lily or Cow Lily

SUNDROPS
Oenothera fruticosa
Evening Primrose Family (Onagraceae)

Description: The lanceolate, slightly toothed, dark green leaves alternate on the stem of this 1–3' plant. The 1–2", 4-petal, yellow flowers are open in the day and have the distinguishing cross-shaped stigma of this family of plants.

Bloom Season: May–August

Habitat/Range: In moist and dry areas from Nova Scotia to Michigan and south to Florida and Oklahoma.

Comments: Evening Primroses and Sundrops form a large genus that has been extensively studied by botanists who have shown that the plants hybridize and form local groups that have slightly different characteristics. For the purpose of a simple positive identification of the genus, the plants can be divided into 2 large groups. Plants whose flowers open at twilight are the Evening Primroses, and plants whose flowers are open during the day are Sundrops.

Sundrops

YELLOW LADY'S SLIPPER
Cypripedium calceolus
Orchid Family (Orchidaceae)

Description: The elongated, ovate leaves alternate on the stem of this 8–12" plant. The 1–2" yellow flowers have an open pouch. The lateral petals are usually twisted.

Bloom Season: April–July

Habitat/Range: In bogs, swamps, and woodlands from Newfoundland to British Columbia and south to New Jersey, the mountains of Georgia and Tennessee, Missouri, Texas, New Mexico, and Washington.

Comments: This Lady's Slipper is at home on mountains and in northern climates. It is rarer than the Pink Lady's Slipper in both the Central and Southern Appalachian Mountains. Its botanical name means Aphrodite's slipper. It blooms for a few weeks at the end of May on Blue Mountain in Virginia.

Yellow Lady's Slipper

Squawroot

SQUAWROOT
Conopholis americana
Broomrape Family (Orobanchaceae)

Description: This 4–8" parasitic plant has no leaves and resembles an upright pinecone. The ½" yellowish flowers grow beneath the brownish scales.

Bloom Season: April–June

Habitat/Range: In rich woods, at the base of trees, from Maine to Ontario and south to Florida and Michigan.

Comments: Squawroot is a parasite on the roots of trees, particularly oak trees. During times of drought, fewer plants come up in the affected woodland.

YELLOW WOOD SORREL
Oxalis stricta
Wood-Sorrel Family (Oxalidaceae)

Description: The 3 leaves have 3 rounded leaflets that bend in half at dusk and flatten when the sun shines. The leaves alternate on the stem of this 3–8" plant. The ¼–½" flowers have 5 yellow petals.

Bloom Season: May–September

Habitat/Range: In woods and fields from Nova Scotia to Wyoming and Colorado and south to Florida.

Comments: Another small yellow wood sorrel *(Oxalis europaea)* grows in the Appalachian Mountains. It can easily be distinguished from the Yellow Wood Sorrel only when the seed pods appear. Only the seed pods of *Oxalis stricta* are bent downward from the stem.

Yellow Wood Sorrel

Celandine

CELANDINE
Chelidonium majus
Poppy Family (Papaveraceae)

Description: The leaves are divided into lobed leaflets. The leaves alternate on the stem of this 1–2' plant. The ¾–1" flowers have 4 yellow petals.

Bloom Season: May–June

Habitat/Range: In moist soils from Maine to Pennsylvania and in North Carolina.

Comments: Celandines are native to Europe and were once used medicinally. Queen Elizabeth I reportedly removed a rotten tooth with an application of the powdered root.

Moneywort or Creeping Loosestrife

MONEYWORT OR CREEPING LOOSESTRIFE
Lysimachia nummularia
Primrose Family (Primulaceae)

Description: The almost round, entire leaves are opposite each other on the stem of this creeping plant. The 1" flowers have 5 bright yellow petals.

Bloom Season: June–August

Habitat/Range: In moist places from Newfoundland to Ontario and south to Georgia.

Comments: The "money" refers to the 2 coin-shaped leaves opposite each other on the stem. The plant is a native of Europe and is still grown in gardens.

YELLOW WHORLED LOOSESTRIFE
Lysimachia quadrifolia
Primrose Family (Primulaceae)

Description: The tapering, lanceolate leaves form whorls of 4 or 5 on the stem of this 10–18" plant. The ¾–1" yellow flowers have 5 petals and grow on long stalks.

Bloom Season: June–August

Habitat/Range: In thickets and open woods from New Brunswick to Ontario and south to Tennessee and Georgia.

Comments: Yellow Fringed Loosestrife *(Lysimachia ciliata)*, a similar plant with ovate leaves and yellow flowers with pointed, notched petals, is found in both the Northern and Central Appalachian Mountains.

Yellow Whorled Loosestrife

Marsh Marigold or Cowslip

MARSH MARIGOLD OR COWSLIP
Caltha palustris
Buttercup Family (Ranunculaceae)

Description: The heart-shaped, glossy leaves alternate on the stem of this 8–24" plant. The 1–1½" flowers have 5–9 bright yellow petals.

Bloom Season: April–June

Habitat/Range: A plant of wet places often found at the edge of small streambeds from Newfoundland to South Carolina and west to Saskatchewan and Nebraska.

Comments: Where the plant is more often called Cowslip, the leaves are eaten as a spring vegetable. The first sign of all greening in the Appalachian Mountains of northern Pennsylvania is along the streams. Marsh Marigold grows along these streams and is one of the earliest blooming plants in this region.

Kidneyleaf Buttercup or Small-Flowered Crowfoot

KIDNEYLEAF BUTTERCUP OR SMALL-FLOWERED CROWFOOT
Ranunculus abortivus
Buttercup Family (Ranunculaceae)

Description: At the base of the plant is a kidney-shaped leaf. The toothed and lobed stem leaves alternate on the stem of this 6–18" plant. The ¼" flowers have very small yellow petals.

Bloom Season: April–June

Habitat/Range: In woods and moist grounds from Labrador and Nova Scotia south to Florida.

Comments: Although the flower is very small, the plant is often noticed because it is among the earliest fairly tall plants to bloom in the woods.

COMMON BUTTERCUP OR TALL BUTTERCUP
Ranunculus acris
Buttercup Family (Ranunculaceae)

Description: The leaves are divided into 5–7 finely divided lobes. The leaves alternate on the stem of this 2–3' plant. The ¾–1½" yellow, shiny flowers have 5–7 petals.

Bloom Season: May–September

Habitat/Range: In fields, meadows, and open woodlands from Newfoundland to Virginia and in Missouri and British Columbia.

Comments: A naturalized plant from Europe, this is the buttercup of the ancient child's game of finding out if someone likes butter. Just hold this shiny buttercup under the chin of someone on a sunny day, and if there is a yellow reflection, the person likes butter.

Common Buttercup or Tall Buttercup

HISPID BUTTERCUP OR HAIRY BUTTERCUP
Ranunculus hispidus
Buttercup Family (Ranunculaceae)

Description: The leaves are divided into 3 toothed segments. The leaves alternate on the stem of this 1–2' plant. The 5 small yellow petals are longer than they are wide.

Bloom Season: March–June

Habitat/Range: In dry woods and meadows from Vermont and Ontario to North Dakota and south to Georgia and Arkansas.

Comments: One of the few buttercups that favors dry woods, this plant often grows in areas that flood only when there are very big storms. The family name of all buttercups is Ranunculaceae, which means "little frog." The name comes about because most buttercups are found in wet places, or like this one, in occasionally wet places.

Hispid Buttercup or Hairy Buttercup

AGRIMONY
Agrimonia gryposepala
Rose Family (Rosaceae)

Description: The divided leaves are the most distinctive characteristic of this 4–8" plant. The leaflets are toothed ovals. The large leaflets diminish in size toward the end, and large and very small leaflets alternate. Several small, yellow flowers, each with 5 symmetric petals, climb a slender spike. The stems are downy.

Bloom Season: June–September

Habitat/Range: The plant is found at the edge of woods and thickets from Quebec to North Dakota and south to Georgia and Kansas.

Comments: Agrimony or agrimonia is an old Greek name for a wound in the eye, which this plant was supposed to cure. The small burs of this plant stick to clothes.

Agrimony

Indian Strawberry

INDIAN STRAWBERRY
Dushesnea indica
Rose Family (Rosaceae)

Description: The 3 toothed leaflets are at the base of this creeping plant. The ½–¾" flowers have 5 yellow petals and 5 green bracts below the petals.

Bloom Season: April–June

Habitat/Range: In open woods and fields from New York to Iowa south to Florida.

Comments: The fruit looks like a wild strawberry, but it is tasteless. There is another yellow-flowered strawberry that grows in the Appalachian Mountains called the Barren Strawberry *(Waldsteinia fragarioides)*. It is similar in appearance, but the flower petals do not have the green bracts of the Indian Strawberry beneath them. The fruit of the Barren Strawberry is dry and inedible.

YELLOW AVENS
Geum aleppicum
Rose Family (Rosaceae)

Description: The divided and toothed leaves alternate on the stem of this 2–4' plant, and each lower set of leaflets is usually smaller than the one above. The 1" flowers have 5 yellow petals and a bristly center disk.

Bloom Season: May–August

Habitat/Range: A plant of meadows, thickets, and wooded areas, from Quebec to British Columbia and south to New Jersey, Indiana, and New Mexico.

Comments: The species name of the plant, *aleppicum,* comes from the name of a town in Syria. Avens are among the few plants that flower along trails in the shaded woods of summer in the Appalachian Mountains.

Yellow Avens

Dwarf Cinquefoil

DWARF CINQUEFOIL
Potentilla canadensis
Rose Family (Rosaceae)

Description: The leaves have 5 leaflets with teeth only on their upper half. The leaves are at the base of this spreading low plant. The ¼–½" yellow flowers have 5 petals.

Bloom Season: April–June

Habitat/Range: In poor soil from Maine to Ontario and south to Georgia and Ohio. Often found along trails and roadsides.

Comments: At first glance Dwarf Cinquefoil *(Potentilla canadensis)* and Common Cinquefoil *(Potentilla simplex)* look very much alike. The only difference between the plants is that Common Cinquefoil leaflets have teeth from top to bottom. The name cinquefoil in both plants refers to the fact that the leaves have 5 leaflets and the flowers have 5 petals.

Shrubby Cinquefoil

SHRUBBY CINQUEFOIL
Potentilla fruticosa
Rose Family (Rosaceae)

Description: The leaves of this 1–4' shrub are made up of 5 toothed leaflets. The ¾", bright yellow flowers have 5 ovate petals.

Bloom Season: June–September

Habitat/Range: In swamps or moist rocky places from Labrador to Alaska and south to New Jersey, Illinois, and Minnesota. Also in the Sierra Nevada and Rocky Mountains.

Comments: This plant is often cultivated and can be found in gardens as a border plant.

ROUGH-FRUITED CINQUEFOIL OR SULPHUR CINQUEFOIL
Potentilla recta
Rose Family (Rosaceae)

Description: The leaves have 5–7 toothed leaflets. The leaves alternate on the stem of this 1–2' plant. The ½–¾" flowers have 5 pale yellow, notched petals.

Bloom Season: June–September

Habitat/Range: In fields and on roadsides from Maine to Ontario and south to Virginia and Michigan.

Rough-Fruited Cinquefoil or Sulphur Cinquefoil

Comments: This cinquefoil, which is native to Asia and came to North America from Europe, breaks all the rules of the other cinquefoils found in the Appalachian Mountains. Cinquefoil means 5 leaves, and all cinquefoils except this one have their leaf broken up into 5 parts. Rough-Fruited Cinquefoil can have up to 7 leaflets. It has the name Sulphur Cinquefoil because unlike all the other bright yellow Cinquefoils, its petals are closer to the light yellow of sulphur.

YELLOW CORYDALIS
Corydalis flavula
Snapdragon Family (Scrophulariaceae)

Description: The finely cut leaves alternate on the stem of this 6–16" plant. The ½" yellow flowers have a spur, and the top petal has small teeth.

Bloom Season: April–June

Habitat/Range: In rocky woods from New York to Southern Ontario and south to North Carolina and Louisiana.

Comments: The roots of most of the *Corydalis* species are potentially toxic. A magnifying glass helps to tell one corydalis from another as the flowers are small but have distinctive differences that can easily be identified with a handheld magnifier. The small teeth on the top petal of this corydalis distinguish it from other similar plants.

Yellow Corydalis

Smooth False Foxglove

SMOOTH FALSE FOXGLOVE
Gerardia flava
Snapdragon Family (Scrophulariaceae)

Description: The upper leaves are lanceolate and the lower ones are deeply lobed. Both types of leaves are opposite on the purplish stem of this 2–6' plant. The 1–2", bell-shaped flowers have 5 light yellow petals.

Bloom Season: July–September

Habitat/Range: In open sunny places from southern Maine to Georgia and west to Wisconsin.

Comments: The plant is a parasite on oak tree roots. Many botanists reserve the genus *Gerardia* for a group of plants with wiry stems and slender leaves. They put all the false foxgloves in the genus *Aureolaria*.

Moth Mullein

MOTH MULLEIN
Verbascum blattaria
Snapdragon Family (Scrophulariaceae)

Description: The toothed, smooth, stemless leaves alternate on the lower part of the stem of this 2–5' plant. The ¾–1" flowers are on the upper part of the stem and have 5 yellow or white petals and 5 prominent red stamens in the center of the flower.

Bloom Season: June–October

Habitat/Range: In fields and at the edge of wooded areas practically throughout the United States.

Comments: Colonists introduced Moth Mullein to the United States from Europe. The plant gets its common name because the flowers seem to imitate all the parts of a moth, with the lower 3 hairy stamens as the tongue.

COMMON MULLEIN
Verbascum thapsus
Snapdragon Family (Scrophulariaceae)

Description: The large, soft, velvety leaves alternate on the stem of this 4–10' plant. The ½–¾", 5-petal, yellow flowers bloom a few at a time on a long stalk at the top of the plant.

Bloom Season: June–September

Habitat/Range: In waste places and fields from Nova Scotia to South Dakota and south to Florida. Also in California and Kansas. A native of Eurasia, it is naturalized in most areas and is a pesky weed in some areas.

Comments: The seeds of the plant are a known narcotic to fish. The Navahos smoked the leaves in their pipes, sometimes mixed with tobacco. In ancient Greece the yellow dye derived from the petals served as a hair rinse. Today in some parts of Europe, the flowers are soaked in olive oil and the oil is used to relieve earaches.

Common Mullein

YELLOW PIMPERNEL
Taenidia integerrima
Parsley Family (Umbelliferae)

Description: The leaves are divided into 3 top and 2 lower opposite, ovate leaflets. The leaves alternate on the stem of this 1–3' plant. Each tiny yellow flower has 5 petals. The flowers form a flat umbel.

Bloom Season: May–June

Habitat/Range: In meadows from Quebec to Minnesota and south to Georgia and Texas.

Comments: This graceful plant is the only one of this genus found in the northeastern United States. Yellow Pimpernel can be found along the Dickey Ridge Trail in Shenadoah National Park, Virginia.

Yellow Pimpernel

GOLDEN ALEXANDERS
Zizia aurea
Parsley Family (Umbelliferae)

Description: The leaves are divided 2–3 times and alternate on the stem of this 1–2' plant. The ovate leaflets have fine teeth. The tiny yellow flowers form an umbel. Each flower has 5 petals.

Bloom Season: April–June

Habitat/Range: Along trails, in open wooded areas, and in meadows from New Brunswick to Saskatchewan and south to Florida, South Dakota, and Texas.

Comments: In large colonies along the Appalachian Trail in the Big Meadows area of Shenandoah National Park and on the Pine Creek hiker/biker trail in Pennsylvania.

Golden Alexanders

Halberd-Leaved Yellow Violet

HALBERD-LEAVED YELLOW VIOLET
Viola hastata
Violet Family (Violacaea)

Description: The elongated, heart-shaped leaves alternate on the stem of this 3–6" plant. The ½" flowers have 5 yellow petals with purple lines at the throat of the flower.

Bloom Season: March–May

Habitat/Range: In mountains or hilly areas from Pennsylvania to Ohio and south to Florida.

Comments: This yellow violet is found only in the western section of the Central Appalachian Range. It is not unusual for plant seeds to be distributed by streams and rivers. In western Pennsylvania and Maryland, the water traveling down the rivers and streams eventually ends up in the Ohio River and the Gulf of Mexico. The waters of central and eastern Pennsylvania and Maryland end up in the Chesapeake Bay. This may explain why some plants like the Halberd-Leaved Yellow Violet are only found in the western section of the Central Appalachians.

SMOOTH YELLOW VIOLET
Viola pensylvanica
Violet Family (Violacaea)

Description: The heart-shaped, smooth, toothed leaves alternate on the stem of this 4–12" plant. The ½–¾" flowers have 5 yellow petals.

Bloom Season: March–June

Habitat/Range: In moist woods from Maine to Georgia.

Comments: This very common yellow violet grows throughout the eastern United States. It usually appears in large groups, often growing near the base of trees. Smooth Yellow Violet produces a prominent, fuzzy, white seed pod.

Smooth Yellow Violet

ORANGE FLOWERS

Orange Day Lily

VICTOR MEDINA

Orange Jewelweed or Spotted Touch-Me-Not

ORANGE JEWELWEED OR SPOTTED TOUCH-ME-NOT

Impatiens capensis
Jewelweed Family (Balsaminaceae)

Description: The slightly toothed, broad, ovate leaves alternate on the stem of this 2–5' plant. The 1" orange flowers form a tilted cup with a lip. The flower has brown spots at the bottom of the cup.

Bloom Season: June–September

Habitat/Range: In damp woods from Newfoundland to Saskatchewan and south to South Carolina, Alabama, and Oklahoma.

Comments: Colonists brought many of our wild plants, which later became naturalized. Orange Jewelweed, a North American native, has been naturalized in England where it is called American Jewelweed. The plant is called Touch-Me-Not because when the seed pods dry they explode at the lightest touch.

TRUMPET CREEPER
Campsis radicans
Bignonia Family (Bignoniaceae)

Description: The ovate, toothed leaflets are opposite each other on the stem of this vine. The 2–3", trumpet-shaped flowers have 5 red or orange petals. The stem is woody.

Bloom Season: June–September

Habitat/Range: Moist woods or thickets from New Jersey to Iowa and south to Florida and Texas.

Comments: Although the northern end of the range is normally given as New Jersey, the vine grows in some localities in New England. It can be seen along the Appalachian Trail just north of Pine Grove State Park, Pennsylvania.

Trumpet Creeper

Flame Azalea

FLAME AZALEA
Rhododendron calendulaceum
Heath Family (Ericaceae)

Description: The leaves on this 2–15' shrub are ovate and entire. The 2–3" tubed flowers are usually orange but can have a range of hues toward the red. The 5 petals are flared, and the 5 stamens protrude beyond the petals.

Bloom Season: June–August

Habitat/Range: Dry woodlands from southwestern Pennsylvania to southeastern Ohio and south to Georgia.

Comments: The plant is native to dry North American woodlands but has been cultivated extensively. In the Appalachian Mountains it is most commonly found in the western part of the range from southern Pennsylvania south to Georgia.

Orange Day Lily

ORANGE DAY LILY
Hemerocallis fulva
Lily Family (Lilliaceae)

Description: The 2' long, lanceolate leaves are at the base of this 2–3' plant. The 3–5" flowers have 6 orange petals and are funnel shaped. The stem forks repeatedly, and a bud grows on each stem.

Bloom Season: May–July

Habitat/Range: A hybrid of day lilies from Asia, it escaped from cultivation and is common in the eastern United States.

Comments: Orange Day Lily is found throughout the Central Appalachian Mountains. Each flower opens in the morning and lasts for one day. The buds of the flowers are used in Chinese cooking and produce the same results as cooking with okra, which thickens the cooking liquid.

TURK'S CAP LILY
Lilium superbum
Lily Family (Lilliaceae)

Description: The lanceolate leaves form whorls on the stem of this 3–8' plant. The leaves are smooth. The 4" flowers have 6 flexed petals, which are orange with brown dots and center green edges.

Bloom Season: June–August

Habitat/Range: In swamps, along streams, and in fields from Ontario to Minnesota and south to Georgia, Alabama, and Nebraska.

Comments: The plant is found in wet soils along streams such as Pine Creek in Pennsylvania and on old farm roads like that at Dickey Ridge in Shenandoah National Park in Virginia.

Turk's Cap Lily

PINK AND PURPLE FLOWERS

Maiden Pink

Periwinkle or Myrtle

PERIWINKLE OR MYRTLE
Vinca minor
Dogbane Family (Apocynaceae)

Description: The lanceolate, entire leaves are opposite each other on the stem of this trailing plant. The leaves are shiny and smooth. The 1" flowers have 5 purple or white petals.

Bloom Season: February–May

Habitat/Range: Escaped to roadsides and woods, from Ontario to southern New York and south to Georgia.

Comments: A native of Europe, it is found in wooded areas that are close to current or past settlements. It grows very well in shade and usually will take over a woodland floor, eliminating all other plants. Because of this characteristic there are efforts to remove Periwinkle from some natural areas in order to restore plants that native insects, birds, and animals need to exist in the woodland habitat.

SWAMP MILKWEED
Asclepias incarnata
Milkweed Family (Asclepiadaceae)

Description: The lanceolate leaves are opposite each other on the stem of this 1–3' plant. The ¼" flowers have 5 pink and white petals and form a flat cluster.

Bloom Season: July–September

Habitat/Range: In swamps and at the edge of ponds and lakes from New Brunswick to Saskatchewan and south to Colorado and Tennessee.

Comments: Look closely and it becomes apparent that the petals of this beautiful plant unite to form the distinctive shape of a milkweed flower. The petals form a 5-pointed crown, and from the base of the crown hangs a 5-pointed bell. Among other places, the plant grows along Lake Trail at Hills Creek State Park, Pennsylvania.

Swamp Milkweed

PURPLE MILKWEED
Asclepias purpurascens
Milkweed Family (Asclepiadaceae)

Description: The ovate leaves are opposite each other on the stem of this 1–4' plant. The leaves are downy beneath. The ½", reddish purple flowers form a hooded cluster. Each flower has 5 petals, each with a pointed crown and dangling points.

Bloom Season: June

Habitat/Range: In dry fields and thickets from New Hampshire to North Carolina.

Comments: Native Americans and colonists used the buds and young shoots of the plant as pot herbs for soups and stews.

Purple Milkweed

Common Milkweed

COMMON MILKWEED
Asclepias syriaca
Milkweed Family (Asclepiadaceae)

Description: The short-stalked, oblong leaves are opposite each other on the stem of this 1–3' plant. The leaves are downy beneath. The ¼", purplish or pink flowers have 5 petals, and each petal has a pointed crown and dangling points. The flowers form round, somewhat drooping heads.

Bloom Season: June–August

Habitat/Range: In fields and meadows from New Brunswick to Saskatchewan and south to North Carolina and Kansas.

Comments: During World War II, milkweeds were harvested for the floss on their seeds to produce life jackets and flight suits. The floss was found to be much more buoyant than cork and warmer, with a weight equal to wool.

Dame's Rocket or Dame's Violet

DAME'S ROCKET OR DAME'S VIOLET
Hesperis matronalis
Mustard Family (Brassicaceae)

Description: The toothed, lanceolate leaves alternate on the stem of this 2–3' plant. The ¾–1" flowers have 4 purple, pink, or white petals. The flowers on a single plant are normally one color.

Bloom Season: May–August

Habitat/Range: Escaped from gardens to roadsides and open wooded areas from Newfoundland to Michigan and south to Georgia, Kentucky, and Kansas.

Comments: When Dame's Rocket first blooms in an area, it is a showy plant. Late in the blooming season, the flowers are few and there are many long (up to 5"), narrow seed pods, completely changing its look. The plant probably came to North America with the first English settlers, since it is a common plant of old-fashioned English gardens.

DEPTFORD PINK
Dianthus armeria
Pink Family (Caryophyllaceae)

Description: The grasslike leaves are opposite each other on the stem of this 6–15" plant. The ½", vivid pink flowers have 5 petals with little white dots. Although the flowers are small, they are so bright that they call attention to themselves.

Bloom Season: June–September

Habitat/Range: In fields and along trails and roadsides from Quebec and southern Ontario and south to Iowa and Georgia.

Comments: Deptford Pinks are one of the very few flowering plants in the grasses along the edge of trails or in meadows. There are no native species of *Dianthus* in the United States. Deptford Pink grows everywhere in the Central Appalachian Mountains.

Deptford Pink

MAIDEN PINK
Dianthus deltoides
Pink Family (Caryophyllaceae)

Description: The small, grasslike leaves are opposite each other on the stem of this 6–12" plant. The ½–¾" flowers have 5 dark pink petals that are slightly toothed at the edge with rings at the center of the flower.

Bloom Season: May–August

Habitat/Range: In sandy fields, roadsides, and at the edge of wooded areas from New England to Michigan and south to New Jersey and Illinois.

Comments: It is a native of Europe and one of only two of this species *(Dianthus)* found in wild areas of the eastern United States. Alpine Pink *(Dianthus alpinus),* commonly found in rock gardens, looks like a dwarf version of Maiden Pink.

Maiden Pink

Bouncing Bet or Soapwort

BOUNCING BET OR SOAPWORT
Saponaria officinalis
Pink Family (Caryophyllaceae)

Description: The entire leaves are opposite each other on the stem of this 1–2' plant. The 1" flowers have 5 white or pink petals at the end of a tube.

Bloom Season: May–October

Habitat/Range: In open and undeveloped spaces. The plant is native to Europe and escaped from gardens. It is found in most areas of the eastern United States.

Comments: The crushed roots and leaves make a soaplike lather. In Europe the plant was used medicinally in the form of a tea, but large doses can be poisonous.

Great Burdock

GREAT BURDOCK
Arctium lappa
Composite Family (Compositae)

Description: The ovate leaves alternate on the stem of this 3–8' coarse plant. The 1–1 ½" purple flowers form tufts at the top of a bur.

Bloom Season: July

Habitat/Range: In open and undeveloped spaces from Ontario to southern New York and Pennsylvania.

Comments: A plant similar in appearance but smaller in total size and with smaller flowers and leaves, Common Burdock *(Arctium minus),* also grows in the Central Appalachian Mountains.

NEW YORK ASTER
Aster novae belgii
Composite Family (Compositae)

Description: The narrow, lanceolate leaves have some teeth and do not clasp the stem. The leaves alternate on the stem of this 1–4' plant. The 1–1½" flowers have many purple petals and a yellow disk.

Bloom Season: August–September

Habitat/Range: In fields and along the edges of swamps, streams, and coasts from Newfoundland to Georgia.

New York Aster

Comments: Many wild asters are small plants that are easily overlooked. New York Aster is a very showy plant that can be mistaken for New England Asters *(Aster novae-angliae).* The leaves of the New England Aster clasp the stem and have no teeth. New York Asters can be found in the Catskill Mountains of New York at North Lake.

NEW ENGLAND ASTER

Aster novae-angliae
Composite Family (Compositae)

Description: The lanceolate leaves deeply clasp the stem. The many long, narrow, entire leaves alternate on the stem of this 3–6' plant. The 1–2" showy flowers are purple or rose with a yellow disk.

Bloom Season: August–October

Habitat/Range: In fields and along the edges of swamps and streams from Quebec to Georgia and in Colorado.

Comments: Found along Pine Creek and in Hills Creek State Park in Pennsylvania. New England Aster is often cultivated for gardens.

New England Aster

Purple-Stemmed Aster

PURPLE-STEMMED ASTER

Aster puniceus
Composite Family (Compositae)

Description: The toothed, tapering, alternating leaves clasp the purplish stem of this 2–7' plant. The ½–1" flowers have purple or lilac rays.

Bloom Season: August–October

Habitat/Range: Common in swamps and low thickets from Newfoundland to Georgia.

Comments: Found near the lake at Hills Creek State Park in Pennsylvania, at North Lake in the Catskills of New York, and on the farm trail in the Dickey Ridge area of Shenandoah National Park in Virginia.

Nodding Thistle or Musk Thistle

NODDING THISTLE OR MUSK THISTLE

Carduus nutans
Composite Family (Compositae)

Description: The leaves—deeply cut and extremely prickly—alternate on the stem of this 1–6' plant. The 2–3"-wide, tufted head flowers are dark pink or purple and distinctly nodding.

Bloom Season: June–September

Habitat/Range: In open, sunny places from New Brunswick to northern Virginia.

Comments: Nodding Thistle is native to Europe and has been naturalized in parts of North America. Some botanists do not separate Nodding Thistle into its own genus but include it with the genus *Cirsium.*

SPOTTED KNAPWEED
Centaurea maculosa
Composite Family (Compositae)

Description: The divided, fernlike leaves alternate on the stem of this 1–3' roadside plant. The 1–1½" flowers form purple or pink heads.

Bloom Season: July–October

Habitat/Range: In open areas from Massachusetts to Virginia.

Comments: At least two other knapweeds grow in the Central Appalachian Mountains—Black Knapweed or Hardheads *(Centaurea nigra)* and Brown Knapweed *(Centaurea jacea)*. The flowers on both plants are similar to Spotted Knapweed, but both of these plants have lanceolate, entire leaves.

Spotted Knapweed

Canada Thistle

CANADA THISTLE
Cirsium arvense
Composite Family (Compositae)

Description: The toothed leaves alternate on the stem of this 1–5' plant. The leaves have thorns on the margins. The 2", pink or pale purple flowers form small tufts.

Bloom Season: July–September

Habitat/Range: In fields and open and undeveloped spaces from Newfoundland to North Carolina and from British Columbia to Nebraska and Utah.

Comments: The plant is native to Europe. In some locations in North America, Canada Thistle has become a pesky weed.

Field Thistle

FIELD THISTLE
Cirsium discolor
Composite Family (Compositae)

Description: The deeply cut, spiny leaves alternate on the stem of this 3–9' plant and look as if they have white wool on their undersides. The 1½–2" flowers form a pink or light purple head that is broader than that of most of the common thistles.

Bloom Season: July–November

Habitat/Range: In fields and open woods from New Brunswick to Ontario and south to Georgia and Minnesota, Nebraska, and Missouri.

Comments: From summer to fall, those on the Appalachian Trail from Georgia to Maine will probably notice the Field Thistles in the woods. Its fluffy, bright head stands out among the cool greens, and the flowers are often surrounded by hovering white butterflies.

BULL THISTLE
Cirsium vulgare
Composite Family (Compositae)

Description: The divided, prickly leaves alternate on the stem of this 3–6' prickly plant. The bracts are all tipped with spines, and the stem has spines. The 2–3" flowers are purple or pink and form heads.

Bloom Season: August–September

Habitat/Range: In fields and open and undeveloped waste spaces from Newfoundland to Georgia and also in Minnesota, Oregon, and California. A native of Europe, it has spread to Asia.

Comments: This plant is a biennial. One year it simply produces a flat rosette of leaves. The next year the flowering stem can be up to 6' tall.

Bull Thistle

PURPLE CONEFLOWER
Echinacea purpurea
Composite Family (Compositae)

Description: The broad, lanceolate, slightly toothed leaves alternate on the stem of this 2–4' plant. The 3–4" flowers have a bristly disk and many purple petals.

Bloom Season: June–September

Habitat/Range: In moist rich soils from Pennsylvania to Georgia.

Comments: Because a popular extract of this plant is used as an herbal remedy to ward off colds, it is possible that now more people recognize the botanical name of this plant, *Echinacea,* than the common name, Purple Coneflower.

Purple Coneflower

BLUE BONESET OR MISTFLOWER
Eupatorium coelestinum
Composite Family (Compositae)

Description: The egg-shaped, almost triangular toothed leaves are opposite each other on the stem of this 1–2' plant. The ¼", blue or violet flowers form a flat cluster.

Bloom Season: July–October

Habitat/Range: In moist soils from New Jersey to Florida and also in the prairie states, the Ozarks, and Texas.

Comments: The flowers resemble a cultivated plant from Mexico called Ageratum *(Ageratum houstonianum),* and the plant is sometimes called by that name. Mistflowers also grow in the West Indies.

Blue Boneset or Mistflower

Hollow Joe-Pye Weed or Trumpetweed

HOLLOW JOE-PYE WEED OR TRUMPETWEED
Eupatorium fistulosum
Composite Family (Compositae)

Description: The toothed, lanceolate leaves have a single vein and form whorls of 4–7 on the stem of this 2–7' plant. The tiny, pink or purple flowers form a domed cluster.

Bloom Season: August–September

Habitat/Range: In moist, open places from New Brunswick south to Georgia.

Comments: Another joe-pye weed with a domed cluster of pink to purplish flowers, Sweet Joe-Pye Weed, or Sweet-Scented Joe-Pye Weed *(Eupatorium purpureum),* also grows in the Appalachian Mountains. Sweet Joe-Pye Weed has only 3 or 4 leaves in the whorl, and the plant smells like vanilla when it is bruised.

SPOTTED JOE-PYE WEED
Eupatorium maculatum
Composite Family (Compositae)

Description: The lanceolate, toothed leaves form a whorl of 4 or 5 on the stem of this 2–5' plant. The tiny pink or purple flowers form a flat top cluster.

Bloom Season: August–September

Habitat/Range: In moist soils from Newfoundland to Maryland and in the Great Smoky Mountains.

Comments: Many reference books list the southern range for Spotted Joe-Pye Weed as New York. The plant is very common at all elevations in the Smoky Mountain range of the Southern Appalachian Mountains and on the Piedmont in Maryland. This may mean that climates are changing, or it can simply mean the plants were never reported to botanical authorities from those locations.

Spotted Joe-Pye Weed

BLAZING STAR
Liatris scariosa
Composite Family (Compositae)

Description: The lanceolate leaves alternate on the stem of this 1–4' plant. The bottom leaves can be up to 2" in width, which is unusual for *Liatris*. The purple flowers form dense heads about 2–3" wide. The green bracts of the plant have a thin, colored—usually purple—edge.

Bloom Season: August

Habitat/Range: In dry woodlands of the Appalachian Mountains from Maine to Northern Virginia.

Comments: Found on the Appalachian Mountain Trail around the central section of Shenandoah National Park, Virginia. There are several plants of the *Liatris* genus in the Appalachian Mountains, and this Blazing Star is probably among the most showy.

Blazing Star

SCOTCH THISTLE
Onopordum acanthium
Composite Family (Compositae)

Description: The spiny leaves alternate on the stem of this 2–4' plant. The 1–1½" flower heads are pink with white at their base.

Bloom Season: August–September

Habitat/Range: In open places from Nova Scotia and Ontario to New Jersey, Pennsylvania, and Michigan. Naturalized from Europe.

Comments: Although this thistle grows throughout the range of the Central Appalachian Mountains, it is not as common as Field Thistle *(Cirsium discolor).* The Scotch Thistle can be found growing along Pine Creek in Pennsylvania. This is the thistle that appears on the crest of Scotland.

Scotch Thistle

Live-Forever or Sedum

LIVE-FOREVER OR SEDUM
Sedum purpureum
Orpine Family (Crassulaceae)

Description: The stemless, toothed, ovate leaves alternate on the stem of this 8–30" plant. The leaves are fleshy. The ¼" flowers have 5 pink or purple petals and form a flat cluster.

Bloom Season: July–September

Habitat/Range: On roadsides and fields. It escaped from cultivation and is found throughout the United States.

Comments: Both the wild Live-Forever *(Sedum telephioides)* and the cultivated Live-Forever are found in Shenandoah National Park. Wild Live-Forever is a much smaller and less showy plant with light pink or white petals. It can be found on rock outcroppings along shaded trails. The more showy Live-Forever is more apt to be found along the rock outcroppings of Skyline Drive in open areas.

Pink Azalea or Pinxter Flower

PINK AZALEA OR PINXTER FLOWER
Rhododendron nudiflorum
Heath Family (Ericaceae)

Description: The lanceolate leaves on this 2–10' shrub begin to grow in spring after the plant flowers. The 1½–2" flowers are made up of a pink tube that expands to 5 flaring petals. Five red stamens protrude from the center of the flower.

Bloom Season: April–May

Habitat/Range: In woods and along stream banks and park roads from Massachusetts to Ohio and south to central South Carolina and Northern Georgia.

Comments: One of the several native azaleas, the Pink Azalea blooms in May and grows in higher elevations in the Central Appalachian Mountains. They also grow along the Appalachian Trail in Connecticut.

Early Low Blueberry

EARLY LOW BLUEBERRY
Vaccinium angustifolium
Heath Family (Ericaceae)

Description: The leaves on this 6–24" small shrub are barely toothed ovals. The ½" flowers have 5 white or pink petals forming stout little bells that cluster at the end of the stem.

Bloom Season: April–June

Habitat/Range: In dry, rocky, or sandy soils from Newfoundland to Saskatchewan and south to Virginia, Illinois, and Wisconsin.

Comments: This small plant is very common in the Northern and Central Appalachian Mountains. The berries—usually much smaller than the commercial varieties and sweet—are blue and ripen from the end of June–July.

REDBUD
Cercis canadensis
Pea Family (Fabaceae)

Description: The heart-shaped leaves are not on this 6–12' small tree or shrub when it flowers. The ⅓" pea-shaped flowers are deep pink or rose red.

Bloom Season: April–May

Habitat/Range: In rich soils from Ontario to New York and south to Florida. Also in Texas.

Comments: In April the blooming Redbuds create a spectacular sight along the highways through the Shenandoah Valley in Virginia. In late May, the Redbuds bloom in Harriman State Park in New York.

Redbud

Crown Vetch or Axseed

CROWN VETCH OR AXSEED
Coronilla varia
Pea Family (Fabaceae)

Description: The leaves—made up of 15–20 oblong leaflets—are opposite each other on the stem of this sprawling plant. The ¼" pea-shaped flowers are pink with purple and white and form rounded heads.

Bloom Season: June–October

Habitat/Range: State and county highway departments sprayed this plant on hillsides in many states in the east, from New England south to Virginia, Kentucky, and Missouri. It quickly took hold and has become a pest in many locations.

Comments: In their efforts to stabilize the slopes above roads, highway departments sprayed hillsides with plants that are quick growing. The slopes were stabilized, but plants such as Crown Vetch did not stay put where they were planted. Instead they found their way to woodlands and formed a solid mat, blocking off the sun and killing the native plants that once grew in those locations. Many animals depend on specific native plants to survive.

Showy Tick Trefoil

SHOWY TICK TREFOIL
Desmodium canadense
Pea Family (Fabaceae)

Description: The leaves, which have 3 ovate leaflets, alternate on the stem of this 1–3' plant. The ½", pea-shaped pink flowers form clusters.

Bloom Season: August–September

Habitat/Range: In thickets and along riverbanks and roads from Nova Scotia to Alberta and south to Virginia and Oklahoma. Also in North Carolina.

Comment: Showy Tick Trefoil gets its name because of the many tick trefoils that grow in eastern North America, this has the most abundant display of flowers. It is one of the more common tick trefoils and grows in large groupings.

NAKED-FLOWER TICK TREFOIL
Desmodium nudiflorum
Pea Family (Fabaceae)

Description: The leaves, which have 3 pointed, ovate leaflets, are at the base of this 1–3' plant. The ½", rose purple flowers are on a 1–3' separate stem.

Bloom Season: July–September

Habitat/Range: In dry wooded areas from Ontario to Florida.

Comments: It is easy to distinguish this tick trefoil from all the others that grow in wooded areas. This is the only tick trefoil with flowers on a separate, leafless stem. Naked-Flower Tick Trefoil grows at the side of the Dickey Ridge Trail in Shenandoah National Park, Virginia.

Naked-Flower Tick Trefoil

WILD LUPINE
Lupinus perennis
Pea Family (Fabaceae)

Description: Each leaf is made up of 7–11 leaflets that form a circle. The leaves alternate on the stem of this 8–24" plant. The 1–2" flowers are pea-blossom shaped and blue or violet. The flowers alternate from the top of the stalk downward for 4–10".

Bloom Season: June–July

Habitat/Range: In dry, sandy soils in wooded areas and on banks from Maine to Minnesota and south to Florida, Missouri, and Louisiana.

Comments: Wild Lupine usually has fewer flowers than its cultivated look-alike Garden Lupine *(Lupinus polyphyllus)*. The flowers of Garden Lupine can be violet, pink, white, blue, or multicolored. Garden Lupine grows wild in large areas of Maine and Canada.

Wild Lupine

Rabbit-Foot Clover

RABBIT-FOOT CLOVER
Trifolium arvense
Pea Family (Fabaceae)

Description: The leaves—divided into 3 narrow, toothed leaflets—alternate on the stem of this 6–18" plant. The 1–2" cylindrical clusters are made up of pinkish, furry, pea-shaped flowers.

Bloom Season: May–October

Habitat/Range: In open places and along roadsides from Quebec to the Pacific Ocean and south to Florida.

Comments: The petals are very small, and the sepals have long hairs that conceal the petals, giving the flower a furry appearance. Rabbit-Foot Clover grows in several open places in Cacapon State Park, West Virginia.

Common Vetch or Narrow-Leaved Vetch

COMMON VETCH OR NARROW-LEAVED VETCH
Vicia angustifolia
Pea Family (Fabaceae)

Description: The leaves are divided into 2–5 pairs of narrow, lanceolate leaflets. At the end of the leafstalk is a tendril. The ½–¾" pea-shaped flowers are purple and usually grow in the axil of the leaf.

Bloom Season: March–October

Habitat/Range: In wet fields and roadsides, in stream valleys, and near lakefronts from Nova Scotia to Florida.

Comments: Common Vetch is very much like *Vicia sativa*, a vetch cultivated for forage.

SOAPWORT GENTIAN
Gentiana saponaria
Gentian Family (Gentianaceae)

Description: The lanceolate, entire leaves are opposite on the stem of this 9–18" plant. The 1–2" flowers are blue or purple and the 5 lobes form a closed, pleated tube. Tips slightly open.

Bloom Season: September

Habitat/Range: In wet soils and on lake-fronts from Ontario to Michigan and south to Louisiana and Florida.

Comments: In many of the state parks in Maryland and Pennsylvania, there are lakes formed by dams. This wet-soil-loving gentian grows along the lakefront at one of these lakes at Hills Creek State Park, Pennsylvania.

Soapwort Gentian

GILL-OVER-THE-GROUND OR GROUND IVY
Glechoma hederacea
Mint Family (Labiatae)

Description: The heart-shaped, toothed leaves are opposite each other on the stem of this sprawling plant. The ¼–½" flowers are blue or violet, and the bottom petal forms a lip.

Bloom Season: March–June

Habitat/Range: In waste places, on lawns, and in the woods from Newfoundland to Oregon and south to Georgia, Kansas, and Colorado.

Comments: Whether or not homeowners know the name of this plant, most consider it a pest if it is in their lawn or garden. The same homeowner seeing this plant through a handheld magnifying glass in the woods discovers that the flowers are beautiful, with the shape and coloring of a small orchid.

Gill-Over-the-Ground or Ground Ivy

Motherwort

MOTHERWORT
Leonurus cardiaca
Mint Family (Labiatae)

Description: The lobed, toothed leaves are opposite each other on the stem of this 1–3' plant. The pink or purple ⅛" flowers have a 3-lobed lower lip and form a circle around the stem.

Bloom Season: July–September

Habitat/Range: In open areas, often near streams or ponds, from Nova Scotia to North Carolina.

Comments: Long ago there was a disease called "Mother," and Motherwort was supposed to be a cure. The term "wort" actually means plant and when placed at the end of the name, it usually means the plant was used medicinally.

Wild Bergamot

WILD BERGAMOT
Monarda fistulosa
Mint Family (Labiatae)

Description: The sharply toothed, lanceolate leaves are opposite each other on the stem of this 1–3' plant. The 1–1½", light purple, tube-shaped flowers form heads.

Bloom Season: June–September

Habitat/Range: On dry hills and in open wooded areas and thickets from Quebec to Minnesota and south to Virginia. Also in the mountains of Georgia and Tennessee.

Comments: In most parts of the United States where *Monarda* grow, this is the most common species. They grow in large groups, and they spread a minty aroma.

PURPLE BERGAMOT
Monarda media
Mint Family (Labiatae)

Description: The lanceolate, toothed leaves are opposite each other on the stem of this 1–3' plant. The 1–2", purple, tube-shaped flowers form heads. The stamens protrude beyond the narrow lip of the tube. The bracts have a purple tinge.

Bloom Season: July–September

Habitat/Range: Along streams and lakes and in moist thickets from New York to Ontario and south to North Carolina and Tennessee.

Comments: Purple Bergamot is widely cultivated and grows wild in New England. In the Central Appalachian Mountains, it grows in Hills Creek State Park, Pennsylvania.

Purple Bergamot

CATNIP
Nepeta cataria
Mint Family (Labiatae)

Description: The toothed, heart-shaped leaves have long stalks and are opposite each other on the stem of this 1–3' plant. The ½" flowers are pink and white. The upper petal is slightly hooded, and the lower petal is made up of 3 hanging lobes.

Bloom Season: June–October

Habitat/Range: In open areas and yards practically throughout the United States.

Comments: Catnip was once cultivated because many believed it had medicinal value. It gets its name from the fact that cats are attracted to its smell. Catnip can be found along Pine Creek in Pennsylvania and along the Appalachian Trail in Shenandoah National Park, Virginia.

Catnip

Heal-All or Selfheal

HEAL-ALL OR SELFHEAL
Prunella vulgaris
Mint Family (Labiatae)

Description: The entire leaves are opposite each other on the stem of this 6–8" plant. The 1–2" purple flowers grow on a cylindrical head. The petals form a hood and a hanging lip.

Bloom Season: May–September

Habitat/Range: In fields and woods throughout North America.

Comments: In the spring the flower head is usually compact and near the leaves on the stem of the plant. As the summer progresses toward fall, many of the flower heads elongate, get further from the leaves, and make these plants look quite different. Heal-All was supposed to cure an inflammation of the throat called quinsy. It was also valued for curing wounds.

Lyre-Leaved Sage

LYRE-LEAVED SAGE
Salvia lyrata
Mint Family (Labiatae)

Description: The leaves at the base are usually deeply lobed and form a whorl. There are sometimes a few stem leaves on this 1–2' plant and these can vary in shape. The 1" flowers form 1 or more whorls of 4 light purple, lipped tubes around the stem.

Bloom Season: April–June

Habitat/Range: In dry, wooded areas and thickets from Connecticut to Illinois and south to Florida and Texas.

Comments: Most of the plants in the genus *Salvia* are tropical and South American. Sage *(Salvia officinalis)* used as an herb for seasoning dishes such as turkey stuffing has red flowers.

MADDOG SKULLCAP
Scutellaria lateriflora
Mint Family (Labiatae)

Description: The toothed, ovate leaves are opposite each other on the stem of this 6–30" plant. The ½" violet and white flowers are in the shape of a hooded tube. All the flowers are on one side of the stem.

Bloom Season: June–September

Habitat/Range: In wet, wooded areas, thickets, and meadows from Quebec to British Columbia and south to Florida and California.

Comments: The leaf shape can vary and the leaves can almost have a triangular shape. The common name of the plant comes from a belief that the plant had an efficacy against rabies. It was also supposed to cure hysteria.

Maddog Skullcap

AMERICAN GERMANDER OR WOOD SAGE
Teucrium canadense
Mint Family (Labiatae)

Description: The toothed, lanceolate leaves are opposite each other on the stem of this 1–3' plant. The 1" pinkish flowers have a long, hanging lip, and the upper lip is cleft with a long horn on either side. The flowers grow in a long spike.

Bloom Season: June–September

Habitat/Range: In wooded areas, thickets, and on shores throughout the United States.

Comments: This is a native plant that is easily recognized because of the uniqueness of the flower shape. Other germanders grow in Europe, but this is the only germander native to the Appalachian Mountains.

American Germander or Wood Sage

NODDING WILD ONION
Allium cernuum
Lily Family (Lilliaceae)

Description: The long, narrow, grasslike leaves are at the base of this 8–18" plant. The ¼" flowers have 6 pink or white petals and form a circular head. The head of the plant nods.

Bloom Season: June–September

Habitat/Range: In fields and on hillsides and stream banks from New York to Minnesota, south to Tennessee, and in the Rocky Mountains.

Comments: Another plant of the lily family, Wild Leek or Ramps *(Allium tricoccum)* grows in the Central Appalachian Mountains. It, like Nodding Wild Onion, gives off the familiar smell of commercially sold onions and garlic and is still gathered and used today. Ramps flower heads are erect, and the leaves, which are broad and lanceolate, do not appear until after the flower bloom fades.

Nodding Wild Onion

Grape Hyacinth

GRAPE HYACINTH

Muscari botryoides
Lily Family (Lilliaceae)

Description: The grasslike, fleshy leaves are at the base of this 3–8" plant. The ⅛" purple or blue flowers have 6 petals and form globes that cluster along the stem.

Bloom Season: April–May

Habitat/Range: In meadows and thickets and along roadsides from New Hampshire to Ohio and south to Virginia.

Comments: Native of southern Europe and Asia, the plant escaped from gardens and now grows happily in Harriman State Park in New York and in the mountains of northern Pennsylvania and Virginia.

GREAT LOBELIA OR BLUE LOBELIA
Lobelia siphilitica
Lobelia Family (Lobeliodeae)

Description: The toothed leaves alternate on the stem of this 1–3' plant. The 1–1 ½" purple or blue flowers have a lower lip that is divided into 3 points with white markings. The upper lip has 2 erect teeth.

Bloom Season: August–September

Habitat/Range: On wetlands, roadsides, and streamsides from Maine to Manitoba and south to North Carolina, Alabama, and Texas.

Comments: The species name, *siphilitica*, indicates that people once believed this plant could cure syphilis. It was supposed to be a secret remedy of Native Americans. It grows in Pine Grove State Park, Pennsylvania.

Great Lobelia or Blue Lobelia

Purple Loosestrife

PURPLE LOOSESTRIFE
Lythrum salicaria
Loosestrife Family (Lythraceae)

Description: The stemless, lanceolate, entire leaves are opposite each other on the stem of this 1–3' plant. The ½–¾" flowers have 5 or 6 purple petals. The flowers are clustered in the upper axils, forming a spike.

Bloom Season: June–September

Habitat/Range: In marshes, wet meadows, and ditches beside roadways from Newfoundland to Quebec and south to Virginia and Missouri.

Comments: Purple Loosestrife is a beautiful plant that is native to Europe. In the Northeast it has become a pest. With no natural enemies and a very efficient pollination system, it can take over an entire marsh, killing off most other plants that are the homes and food for a variety of birds and animals. Along many of New York's state interstates, it has taken over drainage ditches, producing a lovely display all summer.

Pink Lady's Slipper or Moccasin-Flower

PINK LADY'S SLIPPER OR MOCCASIN-FLOWER
Cypripedium acaule
Orchid Family (Orchidaceae)

Description: The 2 elongated, ovate leaves are at the base of this 8–12" plant. The 1–3" flowers have a pink to reddish cleft pouch.

Bloom Season: April–July

Habitat/Range: In dry or moist wooded areas and bogs from Newfoundland to Alberta and south to Georgia, Alabama, and Minnesota.

Comments: Lady's Slipper's botanical name *(Cypripedium)* refers to the sandal or slipper *(pedilum)* of Aphrodite, the Greek goddess of love and beauty who was born on the island of Cyprus. Aphrodite is the Greek goddess of love, and Venus is her Roman equivalent. Since Cyprus has belonged to both Greece and Rome, the flower is sometimes referred to as Venus Slipper. Pink Lady's Slipper can be found at High Point State Park, New Jersey, and Colton Point State Park, Pennsylvania.

SHOWY ORCHIS
Orchis spectabilis
Orchid Family (Orchidaceae)

Description: The large, shiny, ovate leaves are at the base of this 6–10" plant. The 1–1½" purple and white flowers have a white lip. Usually several flowers bloom on the plant at one time.

Bloom Season: April–June

Habitat/Range: In rich wooded areas from New Brunswick to Ontario and south to Georgia, Kentucky, Missouri, and Nebraska.

Comments: Because this plant is often 6" tall, it is a little harder to spot than its larger orchid cousins the Lady's Slippers. It starts to bloom in mid-April in southern locations such as the Chattahoochee National Forest in Georgia and mid– to late May on Blue Mountain in Virginia. It often grows at the edge of woodland trails at the base of a big tree.

Showy Orchis

Garden Phlox

GARDEN PHLOX
Phlox paniculta
Phlox Family (Polemoniaceae)

Description: The lanceolate, entire leaves are opposite each other on the stem of this 2–3' plant. The 1–1½" flowers have 5 magenta or pink petals.

Bloom Season: July–September

Habitat/Range: In wooded areas and thickets from Pennsylvania to Florida.

Comments: Escaped from gardens, Garden Phlox usually grows in areas that were settled or are near settlements. Garden Phlox can be found along the Pine Creek (Rails to Trails) Trail in Pennsylvania.

Moss Phlox or Moss Pink

MOSS PHLOX OR MOSS PINK
Phlox subulata
Phlox Family (Polemoniaceae)

Description: The leaves alternate on the stem of this sprawling plant and are divided into narrow leaflets. The ½–1" flowers have 5 white, rose pink, or violet notched petals.

Bloom Season: March–May

Habitat/Range: In dry, sandy, or rocky soils from New York to Florida.

Comments: In the Central Appalachian Mountains, even as far south as northern Virginia, it is rare for plants to bloom in March, but Moss Phlox blooms in March on the Piedmont and Coastal Plain of Virginia and Maryland.

FRINGED POLYGALA OR GAYWINGS
Polygala paucifolia
Milkwort Family (Polygalaceae)

Description: The egg-shaped leaves alternate on the stem of this 3–5" plant. The ¾" flowers are reddish or purplish. The flower has a center tube and 2 tubes perpendicular to the center tube. The side tubes are actually sepals fringed with petals.

Bloom Season: April–June

Habitat/Range: In woods with acid soils from Ontario to Manitoba and south to Georgia.

Comments: This is another spring plant that blooms from mid-April to early May in the Southern Appalachian Mountains and in mid-May to the beginning of June in northern Pennsylvania. Pennsylvania's Colton Point State Park has a picnic grove with a wonderful display of these flowers around the middle of May.

Fringed Polygala or Gaywings

ARROW-LEAVED TEARTHUMB
Polygonum sagittatum
Buckwheat Family (Polygonaceae)

Description: The leaves have the shape of an Indian arrowhead and alternate on the stem of this vine. The ¼" flowers are white or rose colored and form small heads. The stem of the plant is covered with prickles (soft, small thorns), which is why these vines are called tearthumbs.

Bloom Season: July–September

Habitat/Range: In moist soils from Nova Scotia south to Kansas and Florida.

Comments: The related Halberd-Leaved Tearthumb *(Polygonum arifolium)* also can be found in the Appalachian Mountains. It has the same characteristic as the Arrow-Leaved Tearthumb, but its leaf looks like the points of the arrow have been pulled sideways.

Arrow-Leaved Tearthumb

Pickerelweed

PICKERELWEED
Pontederia cordata
Pickerelweed Family (Pontederiaceae)

Description: The heart-shaped, large leaves alternate on the stem of this 1–2' plant. The 1–2" flowers are purple or blue and in terminal spikes.

Bloom Season: June–September

Habitat/Range: Borders ponds, lakes, and streams from Ontario to Minnesota and south to Florida and Texas.

Comments: Pickerelweed grows in northern New York State at the edges of lakes in the high Adirondack Mountains. It is also found on Lake Kanawaki in Harriman State Park, almost as far south and east as the Appalachian Mountains reach in the state. Pickerelweed can also be found both on the Coastal Plain in the north and the south and up on mountains in the south. This large diversity of altitude and climate in the range of a plant is unusual.

Common Ninebark

COMMON NINEBARK
Physocarpus opulifolius
Rose Family (Rosaceae)

Description: The 3 lobed, toothed leaves alternate on the stem of this 3–10' shrub. The ¼" flowers have 5 pink or white petals and form an umbel.

Bloom Season: May–June

Habitat/Range: On riverbanks and in rocky places from Maine to Georgia.

Comments: Early June is the time for a drive in the Appalachian Mountains to see the wonderful displays of flowering shrubs. Ninebark's beautiful pink and white umbels will probably go unnoticed without taking a walk along a trail.

CAROLINA ROSE OR PASTURE ROSE
Rosa carolina
Rose Family (Rosaceae)

Description: The leaf is divided into 8–10 ovate, toothed leaflets, and all but the top one are opposite each other. The shrub grows to 1–3'. The 1½–2" flowers have 5 pink petals and prominent yellow stamens in the center. The stem has 2-pronged, straight thorns below the leaf axil.

Bloom Season: May–July

Habitat/Range: In dry, open wooded areas, meadows, and pastures from Nova Scotia to Minnesota and south to Florida and Texas.

Comments: The pink wild roses that grow in the Central Appalachian Mountains can only be distinguished by small details—the number of leaflets in the leaf or how the thorn is placed below the leaf axil. At least two other pink roses, Swamp Rose *(Rosa palustris)* and Smooth Rose *(Rosa blanda)*, are commonly found in the Central Appalachian Mountains.

Carolina Rose or Pasture Rose

PURPLE-FLOWERING RASPBERRY OR MAPLE-LEAVED RASPBERRY
Rubus odoratus
Rose Family (Rosaceae)

Description: The 5-lobed and toothed leaves alternate on the stem of this 3–6' shrub. The 1–2" flowers have 5 rose purple petals.

Bloom Season: June–August

Habitat/Range: In rocky, wooded areas from Nova Scotia to Ontario and Michigan and south to Georgia and Tennessee.

Comments: Often found in the rocky hillsides above streams and rivers, this plant has edible berries, although they aren't as tasty as other wild raspberries such as the Red Wild Raspberry *(Rubus idaeus)* that grow in the Appalachian Mountains.

Purple-Flowering Raspberry or Maple-Leaved Raspberry

Square Stemmed Monkey Flower

SQUARE STEMMED MONKEY FLOWER
Mimulus ringens
Snapdragon Family (Scrophulariaceae)

Description: The toothed, lanceolate, stalked leaves are opposite each other on the stem of this 1–3' plant. The 1" flowers are on long stalks and have 3 violet or pink petals and a yellow center. The bottom petal hangs down and has a notch.

Bloom Season: June–September

Habitat/Range: In swamps and along lakefronts and stream banks from Nova Scotia to Virginia, and in Tennessee and North Carolina.

Comments: This plant grows in central Pennsylvania at the lakefront at Hills Creek State Park, and along the shores of Pine Creek. The plant gets its name from the shape and coloring of the flower, which reminded people of a grinning monkey face.

Gray Beardtongue

GRAY BEARDTONGUE
Penstemon canescens
Snapdragon Family (Scrophulariaceae)

Description: The lanceolate, toothed leaves have no stalk and are opposite each other on the stem of this 1–3' plant. The 1½" flowers have 5 pale purple petals that have a flattened trumpet shape.

Bloom Season: May–July

Habitat/Range: In and at the edge of dry woods and on rocky outcrops, chiefly in the hills and mountains from Pennsylvania to Indiana and southward to Georgia and Alabama.

Comments: Gray Beardtongue is a common plant blooming in July on many of the rocky outcrops along Skyline Drive in Shenandoah National Park, Virginia.

BLUE VERVAIN
Verbena hastata
Vervain Family (Verbenaceae)

Description: The toothed, lanceolate leaves are opposite each other on the stem of this 2–6' plant. The ¼" flowers have 5 violet or blue petals, and a few flowers bloom on each of the plant's terminal spikes at one time.

Bloom Season: June–September

Habitat/Range: In moist fields, meadows, and along stream banks from Nova Scotia to Florida. Also in British Columbia, Nebraska, and Arizona.

Comments: Although the flowers are tiny and only a few open at a time, the bright color and the plant's candelabra shape call attention to it. It grows in abundance throughout Tioga County, Pennsylvania.

Blue Vervain

Marsh Blue Violet

MARSH BLUE VIOLET
Viola cucullata
Violet Family (Violacaea)

Description: The heart-shaped leaves are at the base of this 6–10" plant on a stem separate from the flower. The ¾–1" flowers are purple. Each flower has 5 petals; 3 form a lip and the flower is spurred.

Bloom Season: April–May

Habitat/Range: In wet places from Quebec to Ontario and south to the mountains of Georgia.

Comments: Violets hybridize and it is often difficult to distinguish one of the many types of violets from its close relatives. To distinguish between Marsh Blue Violet and Common Blue Violet *(Viola papilionacea)*, notice how the petals of Marsh Blue Violet are darker toward the center, and the flower usually grows above the leaves.

Common Blue Violet

COMMON BLUE VIOLET
Viola papilionacea
Violet Family (Violacaea)

Description: The heart-shaped, toothed leaves are at the base of the plant, separate from the stem on which the flower grows. The plant is 4–8" high. The ¾–1" flowers have 5 purple, purple and white, or all-white petals. The lower 3 petals form a lip for the flower.

Bloom Season: April–June

Habitat/Range: In moist meadows and groves from Massachusetts to Minnesota and south to Florida.

Comments: The purple-and-white variety of the common violet is cultivated and is often called Confederate Ladies or Confederate Violet. The word "common" attached to a plant's name rarely means that the plant is commonly found. In the case of Common Blue Violet, it is the most common of the purple violets in the Northeast, but it is never blue.

BIRDFOOT VIOLET
Viola pedata
Violet Family (Violacaea)

Description: The leaves are divided into 5 parts and are at the base of this 6–8" plant. The ¾" flowers have 5 lavender petals that have a yellow center. Some Birdfoot Violets have a dark purple bottom petal.

Bloom Season: April–June

Habitat/Range: In fields, on banks, and in wooded areas from Massachusetts to Minnesota and south to Florida and Louisiana.

Comments: It is called Birdfoot or Crowfoot Violet because the leaves resemble the shape of a bird's foot. This is the showiest of the wild violets, and its most showy form—with a deep purple bottom petal—is more often seen in the Southern Appalachian Mountains.

VICTOR MEDINA

Birdfoot Violet

Three-Lobed Violet

THREE-LOBED VIOLET
Viola triloba
Violet Family (Violacaea)

Description: Three-Lobed in the common name and the species name *triloba* of this violet refers to the shape of the leaves, which have 3 lobes. The leaves are at the base of this 3–8" plant, separate from the flower stalk. The ¾–1 ½" flowers have 5 violet petals.

Bloom Season: April–June

Habitat/Range: In dry woodlands from New York to Georgia and Alabama.

Comments: At the southernmost tip of its range, this violet can be found in April on the nature trail at Fort Mountain State Park in Georgia. On the northern fringe of its range, it grows in early June on the Escarpment Trail in the North Lake region of the Catskill Mountains.

RED FLOWERS

Red Trillium or Wake Robin

Fire Pink

FIRE PINK
Silene virginica
Pink Family (Caryophyllaceae)

Description: The lanceolate leaves are opposite each other on the stem of this 6–18" plant. The 1–1½" flowers have 5 toothed, scarlet petals.

Bloom Season: April–September

Habitat/Range: On road- and trailsides and in woodlands from western New York and southwestern Ontario to Minnesota and south to Georgia and Missouri.

Comments: By mid-April, Fire Pinks appear along the Blue Ridge Parkway near Otter Creek, along the roadsides of Great Smoky Mountains National Park, and in Fort Mountain State Park in Georgia. By May, they can be found in Cacapon State Park in West Virginia. This plant is found only in the western part of the Central Appalachian range.

MOUNTAIN RHODODENDRON OR CATAWBA RHODODENDRON
Rhododendron catawbiense
Heath Family (Ericaceae)

Description: The leaves on this 5–20' mountain shrub are entire, lanceolate, dark green, and shiny. The 2–2½" flowers have 5 red or purple petals and form a cluster.

Bloom Season: June–July

Habitat/Range: In woods in the mountains from Maryland and southeastern Kentucky to northern Georgia and Alabama.

Comments: This rhododendron's range is limited to Maryland and Virginia in the Central Appalachian Mountains. It grows in Catoctin Mountain National Park, Maryland, and on the Blue Ridge Parkway.

Mountain Rhododendron or Catawba Rhododendron

Wild Geranium

WILD GERANIUM
Geranium maculatum
Geranium Family (Geraniaceae)

Description: The leaves are divided into 3–5 toothed lobes and are opposite each other on the stem of this 1–2' plant. The 1–1½" flowers have 5 red or rose purple petals.

Bloom Season: April–July

Habitat/Range: In woods from Maine to Manitoba and south to Georgia, Alabama, and Wisconsin.

Comments: Wild Geraniums are very common in the eastern United States and grow in woods almost anywhere there is even a small woodland. Cultivated geraniums are usually bred to produce many petals while their wild cousins are much simpler plants.

VICTOR MEDINA

Henbit

HENBIT
Lamium amplexicaule
Mint Family (Labiatae)

Description: The rounded, scalloped leaves are opposite each other on the stem of this 4–12" plant. The upper leaves have almost no stalk, the lower ones have long stalks. The ½–1" flowers have red or red purple tubular petals with an upright upper lip and a lower lip.

Bloom Season: March–November

Habitat/Range: In lawns, fields, and road-sides throughout the eastern United States. More common in the South.

Comments: Some of the earlier flower tubes never open, and the flowers fertilize themselves inside the closed tube.

BEE BALM OR OSWEGO-TEA
Monarda didyma
Mint Family (Labiatae)

Description: The short-stalked, lanceolate, toothed leaves are opposite on the square stem of this 1–2' plant. The 1–3" flower heads are red and the petals tubular. The bracts are often reddish.

Bloom Season: June–September

Habitat/Range: In wet fields and along stream banks from Quebec to Michigan and south to Georgia and Tennessee.

Comments: Native Americans made leaf tea from Bee Balm to treat colic and gas. The plants first bloom in early summer and bloom all summer along wet cliffs in Colton Point State Park and along the stream around 100 miles south in Pine Grove State Park (both locations in Pennsylvania).

Bee Balm or Oswego-Tea

RED TRILLIUM OR WAKE ROBIN
Trillium erectum
Lily Family (Lilliaceae)

Description: The ovate leaves are almost stalkless and form a whorl of 3 on the stem of this 6–18" plant. The 1–1½" flowers have 3 petals, which can be red, maroon, or white.

Bloom Season: April–May

Habitat/Range: In woods from Maine to North Carolina.

Comments: These flowers give off an unpleasant scent if bruised. The red or maroon variety is very common in the woods of the Central Appalachian Mountain. The white variety is much more common in the Southern Appalachian Mountains.

Red Trillium or Wake Robin

Cardinal Flower

CARDINAL FLOWER
Lobelia cardinalis
Lobelia Family (Lobeliodeae)

Description: The lanceolate, toothed leaves alternate on the stem of this 1–3' plant. The ½–1" scarlet flowers have a lower lip that is split most of the way into 3 parts. The upper lip of the flower has a split through which the white stamen protrudes.

Bloom Season: July–September

Habitat/Range: In moist soils along stream banks, ponds, and lakes, and in wet meadows from Newfoundland to Virginia and also in Great Smoky Mountains National Park.

Comments: This is one of the prettiest plants growing in the Appalachian Mountains. In Shenandoah National Park off the nature trail at Big Meadows, there is an unusually placed marsh near the top of a mountain where Cardinal Flowers grow.

Wild Bleeding Heart or Fringed Bleeding Heart

WILD BLEEDING HEART OR FRINGED BLEEDING HEART
Dicentra eximia
Poppy Family (Papaveraceae)

Description: The finely divided leaves are at the base of this 8–18" plant. The 1–1½" flowers have 2 dark pink spurs.

Bloom Season: April–September

Habitat/Range: On rocky ledges in mountainous, wooded areas from New York southward and southwest to Georgia and Tennessee.

Comments: This plant is native to the Appalachian Mountains, and it is sometimes cultivated for gardens. The usual garden bleeding heart *(Dicentra spectabilis)* is a native of Asia.

VICTOR MEDINA

Scarlet Pimpernel or Poor Man's Weatherglass

SCARLET PIMPERNEL OR POOR MAN'S WEATHERGLASS
Anagallis arvensis
Primrose Family (Primulaceae)

Description: The stemless, ovate leaves are opposite each other on the stem of this sprawling plant. The ½" flowers have 5 red or orange-red petals. The plants with orange-red petals have a red ring in the center of the plant's petals.

Bloom Season: May–August

Habitat/Range: In fields and open places practically throughout North America.

Comments: The plant is a European native. The flowers close at the approach of poor weather, which is why the English call it Poor Man's Weatherglass. In Irish folklore it is believed to be a magic plant that one only has to hold to understand the language of birds.

Columbine

COLUMBINE
Aquilegia canadensis
Buttercup Family (Ranunculaceae)

Description: The leaves, divided into 3 toothed leaflets, alternate on the stem of this 1–3' plant. The 1–1½" flowers have 5 red petals that form a crown with a yellow center.

Bloom Season: April–August

Habitat/Range: From Nova Scotia to the Northwest Territories and south to Florida and Texas.

Comments: Columbine can be seen in mid-April on the hillsides and rock outcrops that line the roads of Great Smoky Mountains National Park. The same display can be seen around the summer solstice in June on Skyline Drive in Shenandoah National Park and by early July along the roads of the northern mountains of Pennsylvania.

WOOD BETONY OR LOUSEWORT
Pedicularis canadensis
Snapdragon Family (Scrophulariaceae)

Description: The deeply notched leaves alternate on the stem of this ½–1½' plant. The ½" flowers form an array of yellow or reddish bent tubes each with 4 lobes.

Bloom Season: April–June

Habitat/Range: In dry, wooded areas and thickets from Nova Scotia to Manitoba and south to Florida, Mississippi, and Colorado.

Comments: This plant blooms in April in mountainous areas of southern states. From north of Virginia, it blooms in June. The name of the plant comes from the mistaken belief that cattle who grazed in fields where European Lousewort grew would become infested with lice.

Lousewort or Wood Betony

BLUE FLOWERS

Asiatic Dayflower

Vipers Bugloss or Blue Weed

VIPERS BUGLOSS OR BLUE WEED
Echium vulgare
Borage Family (Boraginaceae)

Description: The lanceolate leaves alternate on the stem of this 1½–2' plant. The 1–2" blue flowers have an extended bottom lip and protruding bright red stamens. The flowers bloom in one-sided spikes.

Bloom Season: June–October

Habitat/Range: In open places from Nova Scotia to North Carolina. Also in Ontario and Nebraska.

Comments: Naturalized from Europe, Vipers Bugloss is a troublesome plant in some northern areas. It grows in Pine Grove State Park, Pennsylvania, and all along Skyline Drive in Shenandoah National Park, Virginia.

SMALLER FORGET-ME-NOT
Myosotis laxa
Borage Family (Boraginaceae)

Description: The lanceolate leaves alternate on the stem of this 6–20" plant. The ¼" flowers have 5 blue or light blue petals with a yellow eye in the center.

Bloom Season: May–September

Habitat/Range: In shallow water and wet grounds from Newfoundland to Minnesota and south to Georgia and Tennessee. Also in British Columbia and south to California.

Comments: The plant and the flowers of these forget-me-nots are smaller than the forget-me-nots *(Myosotis scorpioides)* in gardens. The Smaller Forget-Me-Not is a native plant while the other is an import from Europe.

Smaller Forget-Me-Not

TALL BELLFLOWER
Campanula americana
Bluebell Family (Campanulaceae)

Description: The lanceolate, toothed leaves alternate on the stem of this 1–4' plant. The ¾–1" flowers have 5 light blue petals. The flowers are star shaped and have 3 stigma on top of a prominent, long style.

Bloom Season: June–September

Habitat/Range: In moist woods from New Brunswick to South Dakota and south to Florida and Kansas.

Comments: Tall Bellflower grows in Shenandoah National Park from Dickey Ridge to the Pinnacles along the Appalachian Trail and on the slopes seen from the overlooks in Shenandoah National Park.

Tall Bellflower

Chicory

CHICORY
Cichorium intybus
Composite Family (Compositae)

Description: The toothed leaves alternate on the stem of this 1–4' plant. The 1–2" blue or white flower petals have a straight end like a dandelion. The flowers grow on a long, almost bare stem.

Bloom Season: June–October

Habitat/Range: In fields, meadows, and along roadsides from Nova Scotia to Minnesota and south to North Carolina and Kansas. Also in Colorado and California.

Comments: The root of this plant was roasted and mixed with or substituted for coffee. Grown under special conditions by commercial growers, the broad-leaved variety is the high-priced green sold as Belgian endive.

Common Blue-Eyed Grass

COMMON BLUE-EYED GRASS
Sisyrinchium montanum
Iris Family (Iridaceae)

Description: The grasslike, winged leaves enfold the stem of this 6–16" plant. The ½–¾" deep violet blue flowers have 6 petals and a center yellow eye and are visible near the top of the enfolding leaf.

Bloom Season: May–July

Habitat/Range: In fields and meadows from Newfoundland to British Columbia and south to Virginia.

Comments: There is a similar plant that grows in the Central Appalachian Mountains called Stout Blue-Eyed Grass *(Sisyrinchium augustifolium)*. The leaves are wider and the flowers are usually pale blue.

ASIATIC DAYFLOWER
Commelina communis
Pickerelweed Family (Pontederiaceae)

Description: The lanceolate, entire leaves alternate on the stem of this 6–12" plant. The ½–1" flowers have 2 blue petals opposite each other and 1 petal that forms a small white lip. The stamens are yellow and prominently displayed.

Bloom Season: June–October

Habitat/Range: On roadsides, beside trails, and in open, undeveloped spaces from Massachusetts to Wisconsin and Nebraska and south to North Carolina.

Comments: This dayflower is from Asia and is another plant that propagates easily and has become a pest in many places. The Virginia Dayflower *(Commelina virginica)* also grows in the Central Appalachian Mountains but is much harder to find. It looks much like the Asiatic Dayflower, but all 3 petals are blue.

VICTOR MEDINA

Asiatic Dayflower

Bluets or Quaker Ladies

BLUETS OR QUAKER LADIES
Houstonia caerulea
Madder Family (Rubiaceae)

Description: The short, lanceolate, entire leaves are opposite each other on the stem of this 2–8" plant. The ½" flowers have 4 blue or white petals that are at right angles to each other. The flower has a yellow center.

Bloom Season: April–June

Habitat/Range: In open, grassy places or on wet rocks from Nova Scotia to Georgia and Arkansas.

Comments: Bluets grow from a rosette of leaves. Each stem produces one flower, and the plants always grow in clumps. It grows in open areas along the Appalachian Trail in Connecticut.

Lance-Leaved Houstonia

LANCE-LEAVED HOUSTONIA
Houstonia lanceolata
Madder Family (Rubiaceae)

Description: The thin, lanceolate, entire leaves have 1 main vein and are opposite each other on the stem of this 6–16" plant. The ¼" flowers have 4 lavender or white petals that form a small cup.

Bloom Season: May–July

Habitat/Range: In rocky places from Pennsylvania and West Virginia south to North Carolina.

Comments: Botanists cannot agree on the classifications of 3 *Houstonia* plants. Although they all have the same small flowers and leaves as shown in the photo, they have been classified as *Houstonia tenuifolia, Houstonia lanceolata,* and *Houstonia longifolia.* Some botanists think they should all be in one classification while others separate them all or combine them in other ways.

Green Flowers

Jack-in-the-Pulpit or Indian Turnip

Jack-in-the-Pulpit or Indian Turnip

JACK-IN-THE-PULPIT OR INDIAN TURNIP
Arisaema atrorubens
Arum Family (Araceae)

Description: The 3 leaflets are at the base of this 8–18" plant. The leaves are pale beneath. The 3–5" flowers are green and are on the base of the spadix, the club-like feature ("Jack"). The hooded, striped "pulpit" is the spathe. The fruits are bright red.

Bloom Season: April–June

Habitat/Range: In moist woods and swamps from New Brunswick to Manitoba and south to Florida, Louisiana, and Kansas.

Comments: Called Indian Turnip because the root (corm) was eaten by Native Americans after it was boiled. When raw, all parts of the plant contain many needlelike crystals of calcium oxalate, which can cause an intense burning sensation in the mouth and throat. Proper cooking removes the crystals. The dense cluster of scarlet berries is one of the brightest spots on the floor of fall woodlands.

BLUE COHOSH OR PAPOOSE-ROOT
Caulophyllum thalictroides
Barberry Family (Berberidaceae)

Description: The leaves are divided into 3 toothed-at-the-end leaflets. The leaves form whorls on the stem of this 1–3' plant. The ½" flowers have 6 greenish or purple petals.

Bloom Season: April–June

Habitat/Range: In wooded areas from New Brunswick to Georgia.

Comments: Blue Cohosh can easily be overlooked in the woods of Hills Creek State Park in Pennsylvania or along the Appalachian Trail near Milam Gap in Shenandoah National Park. The plant is tall and the flowers are a subtle color, while the forest floor houses many other colorful flowers that bloom at the same time.

Blue Cohosh or Papoose-Root

INDIAN CUCUMBER ROOT
Medeola virginiana
Lily Family (Lilliaceae)

Description: The lanceolate, entire leaves form 2 whorls on the stem of this 1–3' plant. The ¼" flowers usually hang down under the top whorl of 3–5 leaves. The 2 flowers, 1 on each side of the stem, have 6 greenish purple petals in the shape of a dangling bell.

Bloom Season: May–July

Habitat/Range: In moist woods and thickets from Nova Scotia to Ontario and south to Tennessee and Florida.

Comments: The mystery of this plant is why anyone named it Cucumber Root. The root of the plant is white and looks something like a small parsnip or a white carrot. The root was usually eaten raw.

Indian Cucumber Root

SWEET FERN
Comptonia peregrina
Willow Family (Salicaceae)

Description: The leaves of this 2–4' shrub are fernlike and give the shrub its common name. The green flowers form a bur.

Bloom Season: May

Habitat/Range: In dry soils, especially on hillsides, from Nova Scotia to Saskatchewan and south to North Carolina.

Comments: The woods of northern Pennsylvania's Appalachian Mountains have a spicy smell because this small shrub is so abundant. The leaves of the shrub give off this pleasant smell when anything brushes against them.

Sweet Fern

Alumroot

ALUMROOT
Heuchera americana
Saxifrage Family (Saxifragaceae)

Description: The lobed leaves are at the base of this 1–3' plant. The tiny, greenish purple flowers grow in a loose cluster. Each flower has 5 petals and the stamens protrude.

Bloom Season: April–June

Habitat/Range: In the mountains the plant grows from Maryland south to Georgia. It can also be found as far north as Connecticut and Ohio in rocky, shaded areas of the Coastal Plain and the Piedmont.

Comments: Both the leaves and roots of this plant were used by Native Americans medicinally. The leaves were made into a tea and the roots, pounded into a poultice by several Native American tribes, were adopted by the colonists to be used as a topical medicine for skin sores.

PLACES CITED

These are the places where we have seen some of the flowers cited in the text. It is not an exclusive listing since all the plants may be found in many other places in the Central Appalachians and in many cases in other regions of the United States. The state Web sites will lead to other recreation areas in the state. Similarly, the federal agency Web sites will lead to information for federal parks and national forests in other locations.

CONNECTICUT

Appalachian Trail

Location: The Appalachian Trail runs through the northwest section of Connecticut between the New York State and Massachusetts borders. It goes through private land and several state parks and forests.

Additional Information:

For the Appalachian Trail:
Appalachian Trail Conference
799 Washington Street
P. O. Box 807
Harpers Ferry, WV 25425
(304) 535–6331
www.atconf.org

For state parks and forests:
Department of Environmental Protection
79 Elm Street
Hartford, CT 06106
dep.state.ct.us/rec/parks

MARYLAND

Catoctin Mountain Park

Location: Catoctin Mountain lies in the eastern boundary of the Blue Ridge in Maryland and crosses Frederick County in a north-south direction.

Additional Information:
Catoctin Mountain Park
6602 Foxville Road
Thurmont, MD 21788
(301) 663–9388
www.nps.gov/cato

Cunningham Falls State Park

Location: Cunningham Falls State Park is in Frederick County, Maryland, within the stretch of the Blue Ridge that crosses Maryland north-south.

Additional Information:
Cunningham State Park
14039 Catoctin Hollow Road
Thurmont, MD 21788
(301) 271–7574
www.dnr.state.md.us

Washington Monument State Park

Location: The Appalachian Trail passes through this park in western Maryland's Washington County, 3 miles southeast of Boonesboro.

Additional Information:
Department of Natural Resources
Maryland Forest, Park, and Wildlife Service
Tawes State Office Building
Annapolis, MD 21401
(301) 974–3771
www.dnr.state.md.us

MASSACHUSETTS

Pittsfield State Forest

Location: This 10,000-acre state forest is at the extreme western edge of the state just northwest of Pittsfield and at the juncture with New York State.

Additional information:
Commonwealth of Massachusetts
Office of Environmental Affairs
Department of Environmental Management
Division of Forests and Parks
251 Causeway Street
Boston, MA 02114
(617) 973–8700
www.state.ma.us/dem

NEW JERSEY

High Point State Park

Location: This 14.193-acre site is located approximately 7 miles north of the town of Sussex, New Jersey, on Route 23.

Additional information:
High Point State Park
1480 Route 23
Sussex, NJ 07461
(973) 875–4800
www.state.nj.us/dep/forestry/parks/high.htm

NEW YORK

Catskill Park

The Catskill Park is a region of public and private lands covering more than 600,000 acres in Ulster, Greene, Sullivan, and Delaware Counties in New York State, north of Harriman State Park and west of the towns of New Paltz, Kingston, and Catskill, New York.

Escarpment Trail (North-South Lake Campground)

Location: The Escarpment Trail lies within the North-South Lake Catskill Forest Preserve campground which is off County Route 18, 3 miles northeast of Haines Falls, New York, and west of Catskill, New York.

Other Information:
NY State Department of Environmental Conservation
Bureau of Public Lands
50 Wolf Road
Albany, NY 12223
(518) 457–7433
www.dec.state.ny.us/website/dlf

Harriman State Park

Location: This park is in the eastern part of the state, north of New York City on the west bank of the Hudson River, starting at Exit 16 of the Palisades Interstate Parkway.

Additional Information:
Palisades Interstate Park Commission
Bear Mountain, NY 10911-0427
(914) 786–2701
www.nysparks.com/parks

Bear Mountain State Park

Location: Located in the eastern part of the state, the park is on the west bank of the Hudson River, north of Harriman State Park at exit 19 of the Palisades Interstate Parkway.

Additional Information:
Palisades Interstate Park Commission
Bear Mountain, NY 10911-0427
(914) 786–2701
www.nysparks.com/parks

PENNSYLVANIA

Colton Point State Park

Location: Colton Point State Park is in the north-central part of the state in the canyon country of Tioga County. It sits atop the gorge opposite Leonard Harrison State Park.

Additional Information:
Leonard Harrison State Park
RR 6 Box 199
Wellsboro, PA 16901
(570) 724–3061
www.dcnr.state.pa.us/stateparks

Hills Creek State Park

Location: Hills Creek State Park is located in the north-central region of the state in Tioga County north of State Route 6 and halfway between the towns of Mansfield and Wellsboro.

Additional Information:
Hills Creek State Park
RD 2 Box 328
Wellsboro, PA 16901
(570) 724–4246
www.dcnr.state.pa.us/stateparks

Leonard Harrison State Park

Location: This park is located in the canyon country of Tioga County, north-central Pennsylvania, west of Wellsboro, the county seat.

Additional Information:
Leonard Harrison State Park
RR 6 Box 199
Wellsboro, PA 16901
(570) 724–3061
www.dcnr.state.pa.us/stateparks

Pine Creek Trail

Location: This hike/bike trail runs roughly north-south through the Tiadaghton and Tioga State Forests from Wellsboro Junction to Jersey Shore, paralleling Pine Creek. Nineteen miles of the projected 62 miles are presently completed and open.

Additional Information:
Bureau of Forestry
Rachel Carson State Office Building
P.O. Box 8552
Harrisburg, PA 17105
(800) 63–PARKS
www.dcnr.state.pa.us/forestry

Pine Grove Furnace State Park

Location: This park is located in south-central Pennsylvania near the West Virginia border, west of York, Pennsylvania.

Additional Information:
Pine Grove Furnace State Park
RR 2 Box 399B
Gardners, PA 17324
(800) 63–PARKS
www.dcnr.state.pa.us/stateparks

VIRGINIA

G. Richard Thompson Wildlife Management Area (Blue Mountain)

Location: This wildlife management area is in the Blue Ridge Mountains in northern Virginia near the town of Linden and adjacent to a section called Blue Mountain Estates.

Additional Information:
Virginia Department of Game and Inland Fisheries
1320 Belman Road
Fredericksburg, VA 22401
(540) 899–4169
www.dgif.state.va.us/hunting/wma/thompson.html

George Washington National Forest

Location: This section of the George Washington National Forest stretches from a point close to Strasburg southward for some 45 miles along the Appalachians. Along this length it is about 10 miles west of and parallel to Shenandoah National Park.

Additional Information:
Forest Service
Supervisor's Office
5162 Valleypointe Parkway
Roanoke, VA 24019
(540) 265–5100
www.fs.fed.us/gwjnf

Shenandoah National Park

Location: Shenandoah National Park is located in the Blue Ridge Mountains about 72 miles southwest of Washington, D.C., at its northern point and some 91 miles west of Richmond at its southern terminus. Skyline Drive runs the full length of the park for 105 miles.

Additional Information:
Superintendent Shenandoah National Park
3655 US Hwy 211 East
Luray, VA 22835-9036
(540) 999–3500
www.nps.gov/shen

WEST VIRGINIA

Cacapon State Park

Location: Cacapon State Park is a narrow preserve of 6,115 acres situated in the eastern panhandle of the state. It runs from the Virginia border to just short of the Maryland border.

Additional Information:
West Virginia Division of Natural Resources
State Parks and Forests
State Capital Complex, Building 3
1900 Kanawha Boulevard Charleston, WV 25305-0060
(304) 558-2764
www.dnr.state.wv.us/wvwildlife

OTHER SITES

We need to mention two other places where a large variety of wildflowers grow. These living museums are not parks and trails for hiking and recreation, but rather preserves for plants from all over the country.

Bowman's Hill Wildflower Preserve

Bowman's Hill Wildflower Preserve's 100 acres are administered by the Bowman's Hill Wildflower Preserve Association in cooperation with the Pennsylvania Historical and Museum Commission.

Location: Located in southeastern Pennsylvania outside the town of New Hope.

Additional Information:
Bowman's Hill Wildflower Preserve
P.O. Box 685
New Hope, PA 18938
(215) 862-2924
www.bhwp.org

U.S. National Arboretum

The arboretum is a U.S. Agricultural Research Service education and research facility with educational programs, germ-plasm conservation facilities, and display gardens.

Location: Located in northeast Washington, D.C.

Additional Information:
U.S. National Arboretum
3501 New York Avenue, NE
Washington, D.C. 20002-2726
(202) 245-4575
www.ars-grin.gov/ars/beltsville/na

FOR MORE INFORMATION

General Web Sites for National and State Parks and Forests

All Web sites need the prefix http://

Federal Government

National Parks: www.nps.gov
National Forests: www.fs.fed.us

State Government Agencies

Connecticut State Parks and Forests: dep.state.ct.us

Maryland State Parks and Forests: www.dnr.state.md.us

Massachusetts State Parks and Forests: www.state.ma.us/dem

New Jersey State Parks and Forests: www.state.nj.us/dep

New York State Forests and Preserves: www.dec.state.ny.us

New York State Parks: nysparks.state.ny.us

Pennsylvania State Parks and Forests: www.dcnr.state.pa.us/

Virginia State Parks: www.dcr.state.va.us

West Virginia State Parks and Forests: www.dnr.state.wv.us

ADDITIONAL READING

Adkins, Leonard. *Wildflowers of the Appalachian Trail.* Birmingham, AL: Menasha Ridge Press, 1999.

A book about many of the wildflowers along the 2,000 miles of the Appalachian Trail, with pictures and text.

Brill, Steve, and Evelyn Dean. *Identifying and Harvesting Edible and Medicinal Plants in Wild (and Not So Wild) Places.* New York: Hearst Books, 1994.

A guide to finding wild plants and using them for food and medicine.

Britton, Nathaniel Lord, and Addison Brown. *An Illustrated Flora of the Northern United States and Canada, Volumes I, II, and III.* New York: Dover Publications, Inc., 1970.

A comprehensive work in three volumes on the flora of the northeastern United States and adjacent Canada.

Coffey, Timothy. *The History and Folklore of North American Wildflowers.* Boston and New York: Houghton Mifflin Company, 1993.

This book is about the place of hundreds of plants in folklore, history, and social custom, and as food and medicine.

Densmore, Frances. *How Indians Use Wild Plants for Food, Medicine, and Crafts.* New York: Dover Publication, Inc., 1974.

This is a republication of a much earlier paper, "Uses of Plants by the Chippewa Indians," in a report of the Bureau of American Ethnology to the Smithsonian Institution.

Foster, Steven, and James Duke. *Eastern and Central Medicinal Plants.* Boston and New York: Peterson Field Guides, Houghton Mifflin Company, 1990.

A survey of 500 medicinal herbs and plants growing in eastern and central North America.

Foster, Steven, and Roger C. Caras. *Venomous Animals and Poisonous Plants.* Boston and New York: Peterson Field Guides, Houghton Mifflin Company, 1994.

A field guide to wildflowers, trees, and shrubs that can cause toxic reactions.

Gray, Asa. *Gray's Manual of Botany,* 8th ed. New York: American Book Co., 1950

The 1950 edition of this book on flowering plants and ferns of the central and northeastern United States was largely rewritten by Merritt Lyndon Fernall, Professor Emeritus and former Director of Gray Herbarium at Harvard.

Jones, Pamela A. *Just Weeds, History, Myths and Uses.* Shelburne, VT: Chapters Publishing Ltd., 1994.

Descriptions of 30 "weeds" or wild plants, including where they grow and how they have been used by humans.

Lawrence, Susannah, and Barbara Gross. *The Audubon Society Field Guide to the Natural Places of the Mid-Atlantic States: Inland.* New York: Pantheon Books, 1984.

Tours through inland natural sites of the mid-Atlantic states.

Meyer, Joseph E., revised and enlarged by C. Meyer. *The Herbalist.* Glenwood, IL: Meyerbooks, 1993.

This collection lists plants that have been used for medicine, food, dyes, scents, and spices.

Millspaugh, Charles F. *American Medicinal Plants.* New York: Dover Publications, Inc., 1974.

This republication of a book originally published in 1892 lists the uses of plants and their chemical characteristics in treating more than 1,000 ailments. Although many of these treatments are now considered questionable, the publication is of historical interest.

Newcomb, Lawrence. *Newcomb's Wildflower Guide.* Boston, Toronto, London: Little, Brown and Company, 1977.

This popular guide uses line drawings to illustrate wildflowers from eastern Canada through Ontario and south to northern North Carolina and Tennessee.

Peterson, Roger Tory, and Margaret McKenny. *Wildflowers Northeastern/North-Central North America.* Boston: Houghton Mifflin Company, 1968.

This is a field guide for the identification of wildflowers with explanatory text.

Rickett, Harold William. *Wildflowers of the United States, Northeastern States, Vol. I, Part 1 & 2.* New York: McGraw-Hill Book Company, 1965.

This publication of the New York Botanical Gardens is out of print but available in many libraries.

Roberts, David C. *Geology of Eastern North America.* Boston and New York: Peterson Field Guides, Houghton Mifflin Company, 1996.

This book gives the geological features of the lands in eastern North America and geological theories of the processes that lead to their present configuration.

Saunders, Charles Francis. *Edible and Useful Plants of the U.S. and Canada.* New York: Dover Publications, Inc., 1976.

This republication of a 1934 edition discusses edible and useful wild plants in the US.

Wheelwright, Edith Grey. *Medicinal Plants and Their History.* New York: Dover Publications Inc., 1974.

This republication of a 1935 edition reviews the history of herbs and plants in medicine.

GLOSSARY

alternate: A pattern of leaves growing singly at each node of the stem and not opposite each other.

axil: The point at which the leaf joins the stem.

basal: The leaves growing from the bottom of the plant.

bract: A leaflike structure different from the foliage leaves, often at the point where the flower emerges.

calyx: The outermost flower parts. All the sepals together form the calyx.

cleft: A leaf with a deep cut, sometimes to the midrib of the leaf, is described as cleft.

corm: An underground part of stem, like a bulb, whose function is food storage or reproduction.

corolla: The petals all together are called the corolla; the upper, colored, portion being the petals.

disk: The center part of composite flowers like the daisy.

divided: A leaf cut one or more times, possibly all the way to the middle of the leaf, is said to be divided.

entire: A leaf is characterized as entire if the outside margin of the leaf is continuous and unbroken.

fernlike: Leaves that somewhat resemble the leaves of a fern.

head: The dense, short, flowering portion of a plant.

lanceolate: A leaf much longer than it is wide, tapered toward the tip, and widest below the middle.

leaflet: One segment of a compound leaf having several parts.

lips: Sometimes petals appear in an upper and lower configuration called lips, as in orchids or violets.

lobed: Leaves cut but not so deeply as to reach the midrib are lobed.

midrib: The middle vein of a leaf or leaflet.

native: Plants that grow in a region not introduced by humans.

naturalized: Plants that have escaped cultivation or been introduced by humans into an area but do not take over and displace the native vegetation.

ovary: Produces the seeds, located at the base of the pistil.

pistil: The reproductive organ of the flower (containing the style, ovary, and stigma).

ray: The flat, petal-like flowers that circle the disk flowers of a composite.

reflexed: Bent backward sharply.

regular: Most flowers are regular, with petals arranged in a symmetrical pattern and each petal similar to all the others in shape and color, as in the daisy.

rhizome: The stem below the earth, with nodes that produce roots.

rootstock: A below-ground stem.

sepal: the lower part of the flower, below the petals, usually green.

sheath: A structure, possibly tubular, surrounding another part of the plant.

spadix: A stalk in the shape of a club where many tiny blossoms grow.

spathe: A partial, hoodlike covering over the spadix.

spike: A long, leafless stem bearing the flower.

spur: A tubular extension of a flower.

stalk: The portion of the plant attaching a leaf or flower to the stem.

stamen: The portion of the flower bearing pollen.

stem: The main portion of a plant on which grow the leaves and flower.

stem leaves: These grow above the plant base. A plant can have both basal and stem leaves.

stigma: The tip of the pistil that receives pollen.

style: The narrow stalk of the reproductive organ, or pistil.

tendril: A slender part of a stem or leaf whose purpose is to support the plant.

toothed: A part of the plant with a sawtooth edge.

umbel: A growth pattern in which flowers appear in an umbrella shape.

wing: A thin flap at the edge of a leafstalk or along a stem or other part of the plant.

whorl: Leaves growing in a circling arrangement around the stem of the plant are in a whorl.

$\mathcal{I}$NDEX

ABOUT THE AUTHORS

Barbara and Victor Medina are a husband and wife team that has spent several decades rambling through the meadows, woods, and bogs in search of wildflowers. Their searches have taken them from well-known national parks to small ecological gems off the beaten path. They have photographed and cataloged more than 800 wildflowers in the process. They are members of the Maryland Native Plant Society, the Sierra Club, the Appalachian Mountain Club, and the Nature Conservancy.

Barbara Medina has had a one-woman show of her wildflower photographs at the National Arboretum in Washington, D.C. She is the founder and was the first president of the Maryland Native Plant Society. She leads wildflower walks for schools, colleges, and environmental organizations, as well as for the Smithsonian Institution Associates program in Washington, D.C.

Victor Medina has had varied careers as an inventor, research chemist, and director of research administration at major universities. He holds several patents, has served as a book reviewer for special publications within the field of research administration, and was a contributing author for a book on fuel cell chemistry. His is currently the editor of a community newsletter.